TELLING FORTUNES

WHAT WILL YOU BE?
COUNT YOUR BUTTONS,
AND YOU WILL SEE.

RICH MAN,

POOR MAN,

BEGGAR MAN,

THIEF,

DOCTOR,

LAWYER,

MERCHANT,

CHIEF,

TINKER,

TAILOR,

SOLDIER,

SAILOR.

Also by Alvin Schwartz

Chin Music:
Tall Talk and Other Talk

Cross Your Fingers, Spit in Your Hat:
Superstitions and Other Beliefs

Flapdoodle:
Pure Nonsense from American Folklore

Kickle Snifters and Other Fearsome Critters

Scary Stories to Tell in the Dark:
Collected from American Folklore

More Scary Stories to Tell in the Dark:
Collected from Folklore

Tomfoolery:
Trickery and Foolery with Words

A Twister of Twists, A Tangler of Tongues

Unriddling:
All Sorts of Riddles to Puzzle Your Guessery

When I Grew Up Long Ago:
Family Living, Going to School,
Games and Parties, Cures and Death,
a Comet, a War, Falling in Love, and
Other Things I Remember

Whoppers:
Tall Tales and Other Lies

Witcracks:
Jokes and Jests from American Folklore

I Can Read Books® (for Younger Readers)

All of Our Noses Are Here
and Other Noodle Tales

Busy Buzzing Bumblebees
and Other Tongue Twisters

In a Dark, Dark Room
and Other Scary Stories

Ten Copycats in a Boat:
and Other Riddles

There Is a Carrot in My Ear
and Other Noodle Tales

ALVIN SCHWARTZ

TELLING FORTUNES

LOVE MAGIC, DREAM SIGNS, AND OTHER WAYS TO LEARN THE FUTURE

ILLUSTRATIONS BY TRACEY CAMERON

J. B. LIPPINCOTT   NEW YORK

An Acknowledgment

For their generous help I thank the young people at Riverside School in Stamford, Connecticut, and the Winchester-Thurston School in Pittsburgh; the library staff at Princeton University and the University of Maine at Orono; and the folklore archivists at the University of Pennsylvania, the University of Maine, and Indiana University. I also am grateful to Hannah Griff, Kenneth Goldstein, and my wife and colleague, Barbara Carmer Schwartz.

A.S.

Telling Fortunes: Love Magic, Dream Signs,
& Other Ways to Learn the Future
Text copyright © 1987 by Alvin Schwartz
Illustrations copyright © 1987 by Tracey Cameron
Printed in the U.S.A. All rights reserved.
10 9 8 7 6 5 4 3 2

Library of Congress Cataloging-in-Publication Data
Schwartz, Alvin, date
    Telling fortunes.

    Bibliography: p.
    Summary: A collection of traditional beliefs,
popular sayings, and superstitions which also can be
used as games for predicting the future.
    1. Divination—Juvenile literature. 2. Fortune-
telling—Juvenile literature. 3. Astrology—Juvenile
literature. I. Cameron, Tracey. II. Title.
BF1751.S38 1987   133.3   85-45174
ISBN 0-397-32132-5
ISBN 0-397-32133-3 (lib. bdg.)

    The account concerning James Hardy in Chapter 10
is adapted from *Bluenose Magic* by Helen Creighton. It
is reprinted by permission of McGraw-Hill Ryerson
Limited, Toronto.

Contents

What Is Going to Happen?   7

1   Omens   9

2   Love Magic   14

3   Yes or No?   24

4   Reading Tea Leaves   28

5   A Cootie Catcher   33

6   Reading the Cards   38

7   Reading the Hand   46

8   Oracle Bones   54

9   Dream Signs   57

10   Death Signs   65

11   Apollo and the Pythia   71

12   A Crystal Ball   74

13   Your Future in an Egg   81

14   Astrology   83

Telling Fortunes—and Magic   97

Notes   101

Sources   110

Bibliography   118

What Is Going to Happen?

One summer my friends and I began to wonder what life was going to be like for us when we grew up.

We asked daisy petals whether we would get married. We talked about the meaning of our dreams. We sat in a circle around a table knife and asked the knife about the future.

Who among us would be a famous athlete? Who would be very rich or very poor? Who would have the fattest wife or husband? Who would go to jail? Who would die first?

We spun the knife and held our breath. When finally the knife stopped and pointed at one of us, we had our answer. It was exciting, and it was fun.

All of us wonder about the future. It is the biggest mystery in our lives. We wonder about love, marriage, riches, death, and all the other things that affect us. It has always been this way.

When people in the past wondered about the future, they watched for omens. If they saw a shooting star, or heard a dog bark in the night, or had a certain dream, they knew what to expect.

If that wasn't enough, they turned to a wizard or an astrologer or some other fortune-teller. Everyone believed that the gods decided what was going to happen and that fortune-tellers could learn what the gods had in mind. The methods they used were called "divination": learning the will of the gods.

So visiting a fortune-teller was a serious matter. A person would ask his or her question, and the wizened old fortune-teller would stare into the depths of a crystal ball or study the movements of the stars and planets, or use another method, for there were hundreds.

Today we send rocket ships into outer space, but people still use these ancient methods of predicting the future. The more uncertainty there is in the world, the more they use them. Even when people say they are only fooling around, some think these methods just might work.

Can anyone predict the future in this way? According to our modern ideas, the answer should be no. Now and then because of chance, or coincidence, or common sense, a fortune-teller's prophecies do come true. But we can't count on such prophecies to be right.

Yet each of these ancient ways of telling the future does take us into a future world. Trying out these methods is a fascinating game. Not only is it fun, but it also starts us thinking about all of the exciting, and scary, and silly things that may lie ahead.

Alvin Schwartz

— 1 —
Omens

Everywhere you turn there are omens, or signs, of what you can expect to happen in the future. Although they occur by chance, they seem to give you information you could not learn in any other way. In the past people believed omens were not accidents. They were messages from the gods.

Since life is unpredictable, people have always looked for omens: how insects, birds, and animals behave; whether a person dropped something, or sneezed, or had a tingle in his or her ear; whether a clock stopped or started on its own.

Some omens are so old that we no longer know why they are omens. Others are brand new, for we still create them. Here are some that people use:

BEDS. If you get out of bed in the morning on the wrong side, it is a bad omen.

BEES. If a bee comes to rest on your head, but doesn't sting you, you will be a big success in life.

BEETLES AND OTHER INSECTS.
If you step on a beetle,
It will rain.
If you pick it up and bury it,
The sun will shine again.

BIRTHDAYS. What will a newborn child be like?

Monday's child is fair in face,
Tuesday's child is full of grace,
Wednesday's child is merry and glad,
Thursday's child is solemn and sad,
Friday's child is free in giving,
Saturday's child will work for a living,
The child born on Sunday
Is fair and wise and good and gay.

CATS. If your cat washes its face, company is coming. If you dream of a cat, you will soon have one—or more.

DITCHES, HOLES, DIRT, AND NAILS.

Step in a ditch, your mother's nose will itch.

Step in a hole, you'll break her sugar bowl.

Step in dirt, you'll ruin your father's shirt.

Step on a nail, you'll send him off to jail.

DOGS. If a strange dog follows you home, you can expect good luck.

EARS. If your left ear tingles, your sweetheart is thinking about you. If your right ear tingles, it is your mother.

FLOWERS. If you see a broken flower in the road, someone you know may get sick.

FUNERALS. If you see a funeral procession, it is a bad omen. If you count the cars, it is even worse.

HAIRS. Wet your first finger and thumb and draw one of your hairs between them. If the hair curls, you will be rich. If it doesn't curl, you will be poor.

HANDS. If you find the letter M in the palm of either hand, it means money ahead, or marriage, or both.

HORSES. It is a good sign if you see a horse standing with its head over a gate.

KNIVES. If you drop a knife, a quarrel is on the way.

LADDERS. If you walk under a ladder by mistake, you will be hanged. If you remember to back out from under the ladder, you will save yourself.

LADYBUGS. If a ladybug lands on your shirt or your dress, you will get a new one.

MOON. If you see the new moon over your right shoulder, you will be healthy during the coming month.

NOSES. If your nose itches, you will soon become angry.

PIGS. If you meet a pig the first thing in the morning, you will have a bad day.

SHOELACE. If you get a knot in your shoelace, it means trouble ahead.

SNEEZING.

Sneeze on Monday, sneeze for danger,
Sneeze on Tuesday, kiss a stranger,
Sneeze on Wednesday, sneeze for a letter,
Sneeze on Thursday, something better,
Sneeze on Friday, sneeze for sorrow,
Sneeze on Saturday, hug someone tomorrow,
Sneeze on Sunday, safety you had better seek,
Or the Devil will have you
The rest of the week.

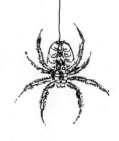

SOCKS. If by mistake you put on a sock or a stocking inside out, it is a good sign. If you do it on purpose, hoping for good luck, no good will come of it.

SPIDERS. If a spider gets into your clothes, it is a good omen. If you see a spider coming down on one of its threads, it is a sign that you will have a guest. But if you kill a spider, you will have very bad luck.

If you wish to live and thrive,
Let the spider stay alive.

WRISTS. If you can make a circle around your wrist with two of your fingers and not touch your wrist, very good things await you.

2
Love Magic

In this chapter you might learn who is in love with you, who you are going to marry, how many children you are going to have, what your life will be like, and when all this will happen. There are many ways to find the answers.

WHO LOVES YOU?

Hold an apple by the stem and whirl it around and around, reciting the alphabet as you do so. The letter at which the stem breaks is the initial of the one who loves you.

Or use this jump rope rhyme:

Ice cream soda, lemonade punch,
Tell me the name of my honeybunch.

Continue to jump, reciting the alphabet until you catch your foot. The letter you reach will be the first initial of the one who loves you.

Pluck the petals from a daisy. In this case you must already have someone in mind. When you pluck the first petal, chant "He [or she] *loves me*"; the second, "*He don't*"; the third, "*He'll have me*"; the fourth, "*He won't.*" Continue until you remove the last petal.

WILL YOU GET MARRIED?

Attach one of your hairs to a ring. If your hair is not long enough, use a piece of thread. Have someone suspend the ring over your head, holding the hair or thread between their thumb and first finger. If the ring swings in a circle, someday you will get married. If it circles twice, you will get married twice. But if the ring swings from side to side, you will not get married.

WHO WILL YOU MARRY?

Write the names of those who are possibilities on separate slips of paper. Include one paper with no name written on it. Place the papers under your pillow. When you awaken each morning, reach under your pillow and remove one slip. Throw it away without looking at it. Only look at the last slip you remove. It will have the name of the person you will marry. If it is blank, you will marry someone you have not met yet.

Count the seeds in an apple or the petals on a daisy while saying this rhyme. As you do so, have someone in mind. The number of seeds will tell you what to expect.

One, I love,
Two, I loathe,
Three, I cast away,
Four, I love with all my heart,
Five, I love, I say,
Six, he loves,
Seven, I love,
Eight, he'll marry me,

16

Nine, he comes,
Ten, he tarries,
Eleven, he courts,
Twelve, we marry,
Thirteen, we quarrel,
Fourteen, we part,
Fifteen, we die of broken hearts.

If this rhyme is too sad for you, here is another ending.

Thirteen, a happy life,
Fourteen, a happy wife,
Fifteen, a lot of fun,
Sixteen, a little one.

Matching names will tell you about your chances of marrying a particular person. Write out the two names in this way:

G E O R G E   W A S H I N G T O N
M A R T H A   D A N D R I D G E

Cross out each letter that is in your first name and the other person's last name. Do the same with the other person's first name and your last name. For each letter you cross out in one name, cross out only one in the other name.

Next, apply the formula "love, hate, friendship, marriage" to the letters you have not crossed out. Use "love" with the first such letter, "hate" with the second, and so on. Do this for each name separately. In that way you can learn what each of you wants.

With George and Martha there is a problem. George hates Martha, but Martha loves George. Friendship is the best they can hope for. Marriage would be risky.

On the night of a new moon, go out of doors and call out the name of the person you want to marry. If when you next see that person he or she is turned away from you, you will not marry. But if he or she is facing you, there is a good chance that you will.

You might marry someone you will not meet for many years, but some say you can see in advance who this will be. The very best time is at midnight on Halloween or on Saint Agnes' Eve, January 20.

Go alone into a darkened room that has a mirror. Close the door, stand in front of the mirror, and brush or comb your hair. As you stare into the mirror, it is said, you will see the face of your future spouse peering over your shoulder. But don't turn around or the face will disappear.

Not too many years ago, in some parts of the United States, a young woman would arrange a strange ceremony to see the man she would marry. It was called a "dumb supper," or silent supper. The woman prepared this supper alone or had a friend help her, for it was a scary experience. Late at night she would set the table with dishes, silverware, and a chair for one person. She might even place some food on the table. Often this was just a small cake of cornmeal called a dumb cake.

As part of this ritual, the woman wore her clothing backwards or inside out and walked backwards as she moved about. She even set the table with her back to it. This was done to thwart evil spirits. All the while, she was not supposed to utter a sound or even smile. As midnight approached, she turned out the lights, stood silently behind the chair at the table and waited. There were always some who said they saw the man they would marry.

If you can bend your thumb back so that it touches your wrist, you can marry anyone you want. This also is true if you can make your first finger and little finger touch over the back of your hand.

WHEN WILL YOU GET MARRIED?

The number of times it takes to blow away the seed head of a dandelion equals the number of years before you marry.

WILL YOU GET MARRIED BEFORE YOUR BEST FRIEND?

To find out, sleep in the same bed with your friend. Tie your big toe to your friend's big toe with a piece of thread. By morning the thread will have broken. The person with the longest piece will marry first.

HOW MANY CHILDREN WILL YOU HAVE?

The number of seeds in a daisy will tell you. With your thumb and forefinger, remove the seeds from the center of a daisy and place them in your palm. Then toss them into the air and catch as many as you can on the back of your hand. The number you catch will equal the number of children you will have. If two or more seeds stick together, it is a sign of twins or triplets or more.

Or count the seeds in an apple, the wrinkles in your forehead, or the wrinkles in the skin covering the bottom joint of your left pinkie, and you will know. Or skip a flat stone across a pond or stream. Each time the stone strikes the water counts as one child.

WHAT KIND OF LIFE WILL YOU HAVE?

To learn what to expect, draw a large rectangle divided into sixteen small boxes like the one shown. It will tell you where you will live, the transportation you will use, even the kind of clothing you will wear.

City	Suburb	Slum	Farm
Big House	Little House	Pigpen	Barn
Car	Airplane	Wheel-barrow	Horse
Silk	Satin	Cotton Rags	Paper Bags

To start, decide how old you are going to be when you get married. Let's say you will be twenty-five. Beginning with the top line of boxes, move from left to right, counting the boxes until you reach the last one. This will give you sixteen. Then go back to the first box and continue counting until you reach the twenty-fifth, which will be "Car." Cross it out.

Starting with the next box, count again to twenty-five and cross out that box. Continue counting in this way, but do not count any boxes you have crossed out. Also skip each line that has only one box remaining.

22

When you finish, there will be one box left on each line. These boxes will tell your fortune.

If you marry when you are twenty-five, you will live in a barn in the city, go around in a wheelbarrow, and wear paper bags. To get other information, just change the categories and the choices.

For another way of doing this, called MASH, see p. 103.

WILL YOUR MARRIAGE SUCCEED?

This is similar to the method of matching names described earlier, but here both a husband and a wife are involved. Write down their names this way using the woman's maiden name:

B A R B A R A   C A R M E R = 10
A L V I N   S C H W A R T Z = 10

As before, cross out each letter that is in the woman's first name and the man's last name. Then do the same with the man's first name and the woman's last name.

Now add up the remaining letters in each person's name. If the totals for both are even numbers, the marriage is likely to succeed. As you can see, that is how things added up for the author and his wife, and their marriage has worked out very well indeed.

⎯ 3 ⎯
Yes or No?

Learning the future may be as easy as selecting a piece of paper marked "yes" or "no." Just write these words on separate slips of paper and fold the papers so that the words cannot be seen. Then ask a question about the future that can be answered with "yes" or "no." Shuffle the papers and choose one to get an answer.

This old method of learning the future is called draw-ing—or casting—lots. There are countless ways to do this, but with each you select the answer by chance. It may seem like guessing, but in the past people be-lieved that some supernatural power guided them to the right choice. With the methods below, just ask a question, then follow the directions.

A WORD. Choose a long word at random, like "ency-clopedia" or "divination." Count the letters. If they add up to an even number, the answer is yes. If it is an odd number, the answer is no.

A HAIR COMB. Choose one of the teeth in your hair comb at random. Starting at the far end of the comb, recite "Yes, no, maybe so," using one of these possible answers for each tooth you come to. When you reach the tooth you selected, you will have your answer.

A PEBBLE. Drop a pebble into a bowl of water. Count the number of ripples the pebble makes in the water. If the number is even, the answer to your question is yes. If the number is odd, the answer is no.

With the following methods, you do not need a question.

A PAGE IN A BOOK. Open a book at random. The first words to catch your eye will suggest what to expect. Any book will do, although often a book of poetry or the Bible is used.

WORDS IN A CROWD. Go to a busy street. The first words you hear will suggest what is to come.

THREE DICE. Roll three dice, adding the dots that turn up. Then use the list below to learn what they predict.

Three	*Expect a surprising development.*
Four	*Beware of a serious quarrel.*
Five	*You will receive unexpected help.*
Six	*You will lose something important.*
Seven	*You will have a problem that causes gossip.*
Eight	*If you follow your plans, you will be criticized and will lose friends.*
Nine	*There is a marriage in your future.*
Ten	*A child will enter your life.*
Eleven	*You will part from a loved one.*
Twelve	*You will soon receive an important message.*
Thirteen	*Make no changes, or you will have bad luck.*
Fourteen	*Beware of a secret enemy.*
Fifteen	*Expect trouble.*
Sixteen	*Expect good fortune.*
Seventeen	*An ordinary journey will lead to unexpected happiness.*
Eighteen	*You will become very important.*

MASHED POTATOES. Children in Scotland use this method late at night on Halloween. Charms, such as those listed below, are mixed into a bowl of steaming mashed potatoes. Each child spoons out a portion, then carefully looks for a charm. The one he or she finds predicts the future:

A ring, the first to marry; a button or thimble, the last to marry or no marriage; a nut, good luck; a coin, wealth; a wishbone, great success.

— 4 —
Reading Tea Leaves

In years gone by you could go to a tea shop and order a pot of hot tea and a chocolate éclair or a strawberry tart. Afterwards a mysterious-looking Gypsy woman would tell your fortune from the tea leaves left in your tea cup.

It is hard to find such a tea shop today, but the method of reading leaves is still the same. After you finish all but a teaspoon or two of your tea, swirl what is left around the cup three times from left to right to distribute the leaves. Then turn the cup upside down on the saucer to drain off the remaining tea, counting to seven to give it enough time.

If a fortune-teller is reading the leaves, hand the upside-down cup and saucer to her. She will return them to their normal position and arrange the handle so that it points towards you. Then the reading begins.

The fortune-teller studies the clusters of tea leaves on the sides and bottom of the cup. Do they look like birds, butterflies, cats, clouds, or something else? And what do they say about your future?

The position of the leaves in the cup also is important. The closer they are to the rim, the sooner that part of the prophecy will come true. Those on the bottom predict what will happen far in the future. How close they are to the handle also is part of the picture. The closer they are, the more likely that you will be the cause of whatever the tea leaves show: a quarrel, a love affair, or some other development. The farther away they are, the more likely that someone else will cause the problem.

In studying tea leaves a good fortune-teller also relies on her intuition and the impressions she has of you.

You can learn to read the leaves yourself. It is best if you brew your tea with loose tea leaves. If you don't have any, cut open a few tea bags and use that tea instead. To make it easier to read the leaves, use a white cup with a large mouth.

There are hundreds of shapes the leaves can form, and each has a traditional meaning. The list below includes many of these. Of course, the more often you read the leaves, the more shapes you will see and understand.

If the tea leaves form...	Its meaning is . . .
an anchor	a pleasant journey
an ant	hard times, hard work
an ape, a monkey	success
an axe, a gun	trouble
a bell	a wedding or good news
a bird	important news, possibly bad news
a bouquet of flowers	good luck
a broom	a fresh start
a butterfly	an enjoyable experience
a butterfly with open wings	a friend in trouble
a capital letter	the initial of a person you will meet
a castle	you will marry someone rich
a cat	a quarrel
a circle	success
a circle with a dot inside	a wish for you to make
a coffin	a death, other bad news
a cross	trouble
a crown	money
a dagger	danger
a dot	money (the bigger the dot, the more you can expect)
three dots in a row	a wish will come true
a duck	happiness

an egg	you will lose your savings
flowers	children
a gate	a change that leads to happiness
a heart	a letter is coming
lightning	happiness
lines: a straight line	a peaceful period
a jagged line	trouble
a moon	love and kisses
a number	minutes, hours, days, months, years; the number eight may mean an important change
a pathway through the tea grounds	a journey
a pig	someone will be joining the family
a question mark	danger
a ring of dots at the bottom of the cup	separation from a loved one
a rowboat	be patient
a snake	a threat or an enemy
a spider	a change bringing happiness
a square	no marriage soon
a star	good luck
a sword	arguments
a triangle	good luck
a tree	good health
several trees	a wish will come true
a wheel	you will inherit money

Note: A cluster of bubbles on top of your tea has nothing to do with tea leaves, but it also may tell something of your future. Each bubble stands for a kiss or for money. If you scoop up the bubbles with a spoon and swallow them before they break, you can expect as many kisses as there are bubbles, or quite a bit of money, or both.

— 5 —
A Cootie Catcher

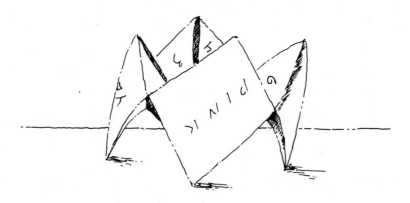

Cooties are little bugs that get in your hair if you don't keep it clean. A cootie catcher sounds as if it could catch them, but its real job is to tell fortunes.

To make a cootie catcher, use a piece of paper at least eight inches square and follow these directions:

1. Fold the four corners so that they come together at the center.

2. Turn the paper over. Fold the corners on this side so that they meet at the center. They will form four triangles.

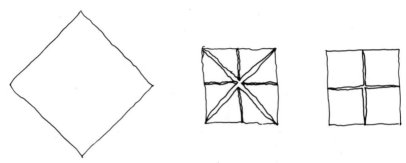

The other side now will have four squares.

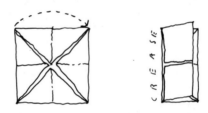

3. Fold the side with the triangles in half from left to right. Make a sharp crease along the fold.

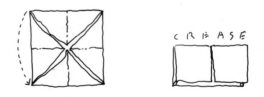

4. Fold it in half again, this time from top to bottom. Make another sharp crease.

34

5. Unfold the cootie catcher to the way it was in step 2. On one side you now will have eight triangles instead of four. On the other side you still will have four squares.

6. Write a number from 1 to 25 on each of the triangles. Write the name of a color on each of the squares.

7. Write a brief fortune on the back of each of the eight triangles. These usually are silly fortunes: "The music teacher loves you." "Expect to fail gym." "You will have thirteen husbands (or wives)."

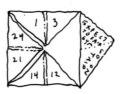

To operate a cootie catcher, follow these steps:

1. Hold the catcher so that the eight triangles are on top and the four squares are on the bottom. Fold the catcher in half, as in step 4 above. Slip your left thumb under one square and your left first finger under the square next to it. Slip your right thumb and forefinger under the other two squares.

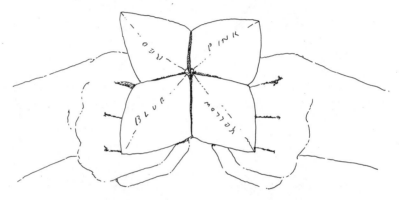

2. To open the cootie catcher, pinch the fold of paper between each thumb and forefinger. Draw your hands back slightly. Inside you will see the numbers on four of the triangles.

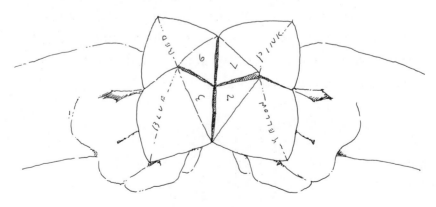

Now spread your thumbs and forefingers, and you will see the numbers on the other four triangles.

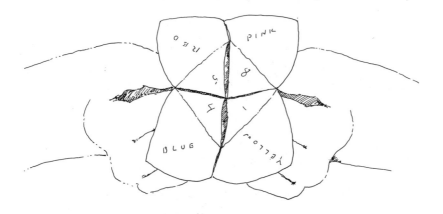

3. To close the cootie catcher, push the two sides together. This will reveal the names of the four colors.

4. To tell someone's fortune, ask that person to select one of the colors. Now spell out the color—G-R-E-E-N, for example. As you do so, make one movement with the cootie catcher for each letter. First open the catcher halfway, then all the way, then close it halfway, then open it all the way, stopping when you reach the last letter.

5. At this point ask the person to choose one of the numbers that can be seen inside the catcher. Open and close the catcher that number of times.

6. Now ask him or her to choose one more of the numbers. Then turn over the triangle with that number and learn what the future will bring.

— 6 —
Reading the Cards

People who tell fortunes with playing cards claim they can tell more about a person's life and future with this method than with any other. In this chapter there are three ways of using cards to tell fortunes. Two are simple. The third is more complicated, but it is the one that tells the most about the future.

YES OR NO

Will you get fat? Will it rain on your birthday? Will your father let you drive the car? To learn the answers, place a deck of cards face down on a table. Ask the question, then turn over three cards. Of course, turning

38

them over slowly increases the suspense. If two of the three cards are red, the answer is yes. If two of the three are black, the answer is no.

A MARRIAGE CARD

If you are a girl, remove all the jacks from the deck. Give three of the jacks the names of boys you might want to marry someday. To make it more interesting, name the fourth jack after someone you would *not* want to marry. If you are a boy, remove the queens and do the same thing. Place the four cards on the table side by side.

Use the 2, 3, 4, and 5 of hearts as answer cards. The 2 of hearts stands for "going steady," the 3 for "engaged," the 4 for "married," and the 5 for "divorced." These cards remain in the deck, but shuffle the deck to be sure they are well distributed.

Now deal the cards one at a time to each of the jacks or queens until all the answer cards are dealt. If two or more answer cards land on a jack or queen, the last one dealt counts.

With this method you can tell a more detailed fortune. Remove all cards from 2 to 5 from the deck. This will give you a deck of thirty-six cards. Divide the deck into nine equal piles of cards.

Remove the top card from each pile. Arrange them face up so that you have a row of nine cards. Use these to tell your fortune. If you are telling someone else's fortune, have that person arrange the cards.

Nine cards are used because nine is said to be a mystical number. Fortune-tellers say that nine of anything add up to something whole. Together the nine cards are supposed to tell of important events and changes in one period of a person's life.

Here are the nine cards a friend of mine drew and what they told him.

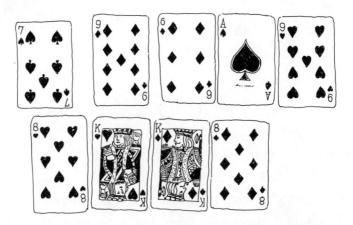

Expect to go through a difficult period. Your marriage may fail, and your business will have serious trouble. However, you will overcome these problems with the advice of a friend and with your savings. Soon after you will enter a happier period. With the help of your father, your business will begin to succeed, and you will fall in love again with your wife.

Each card in a deck has one or more meanings, and some may have as many as four or five. Several are given below. A fortune-teller selects the one that he or she feels best suits the questioner.

Read the cards from left to right in the order in which they are arranged. In trying to understand their meaning, remember that each is part of a complete picture. If you are not sure what a card means, place your hands on it and close your eyes. The fortune-tellers say this will help you to understand it better.

HEARTS

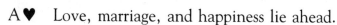
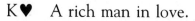
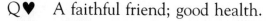

A♥ Love, marriage, and happiness lie ahead.

K♥ A rich man in love.

Q♥ A faithful friend; good health.

J♥ A young man in love who may be a friend or an enemy. You may wish to avoid him.

10♥ A wedding card; possibly a wedding and children.

9♥ Success lies ahead. If you draw this card, make a wish and it is supposed to come true.

8♥ Jealousy or a joyous experience may be involved.

7♥ An old friend arrives for a visit, or a trip leads to romance.

6♥ Someone generous.

41

DIAMONDS

A♦   You soon will receive a letter with money.

K♦   An older man who brings good advice.

Q♦   An older woman who offers good advice; or a harmful woman.

J♦   A letter from a stranger with unexpected help.

10♦   A large amount of money will be yours if you act promptly.

9♦   A good time to make money.

8♦   Success.

7♦   Great success because of the influence of a friend, or a new baby arrives.

6♦   You will have enough money for quite a while.

CLUBS

A♣   Money is on the way.

K♣   A happy man.

Q♣   Go to a woman for advice.

J♣   A good friend.

10♣   An important meeting about the future.

9♣   A death card. Danger or death ahead. Don't make any changes.

8♣   Your job will change.

7♣   A good future lies ahead, or beware of the opposite sex.

6♣   Your work may bore you, but don't change jobs.

A♠ A bad luck card. Death is on its way, or expect trouble in business.

K♠ A lawyer or a trusted friend will try to take advantage of you.

Q♠ A dark, slender woman is working against you.

J♠ Have nothing to do with a young stranger.

10♠ An accident. You may go to prison.

9♠ Sorrow and sickness await you or someone you know.

8♠ Bad news, but don't make any changes.

7♠ Jealousy, or grief and tears. In any case, be patient.

6♠ Death.

SPECIAL MEANINGS.

If the ace of diamonds is next to the seven of diamonds, it means a quarrel. If it is next to the nine of spades, it means illness.

If two aces are side by side, it means a marriage. If three or four aces are, it means great success.

If two or more queens are together, it means gossip about you, perhaps even a scandal. About what? Who should know better than you?

Three or more tens together mean extra money or something else wonderful.

Three or more nines mean unexpected good luck.

THE EMPEROR

THE LOVERS

THE CHARIOT

TAROT CARDS

After you have learned to tell fortunes with ordinary playing cards, try using the mysterious tarot cards. It is said they are able to predict the future with very great accuracy.

The tarot cards probably are the oldest playing cards in the world and are ancestors of the cards we use today. But no one knows where tarot cards came from or when they were first used. Some say they came into being in ancient India or ancient Greece and eventually were brought to Europe by Gypsies. Today they are used in over sixty countries.

There are seventy-eight cards in a tarot deck. All are needed to play the old game of tarot, but only twenty-two are needed to tell a fortune. These are called the Major Arcana, or the trump cards. They focus on our desires, fears, ignorance, or wisdom, and on how these things affect the future.

Each trump card has a picture based on an ancient drawing. It may be a juggler, an emperor, an empress, two people in love, a hermit, a hanged man, or a wheel of fortune. Other trump cards stand for death, strength, justice, and the judgement day. One of the most important cards shows a fool (who later became the joker in a deck of ordinary playing cards). Each of these cards has many special meanings, and there are several books available on how to read the tarot. One book for a beginner is *The Tarot Revealed: A Modern Guide to Reading the Tarot Cards* by Eden Gray.

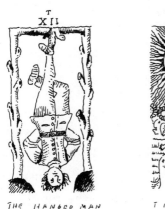  

THE HANGED MAN   THE SUN   THE FOOL

According to an old belief, you should not purchase a deck of tarot cards yourself or you will have bad luck. You should receive the cards as a gift. When they are not in use, wrap them in a piece of silk and keep them under your pillow.

— 7 —
Reading the Hand

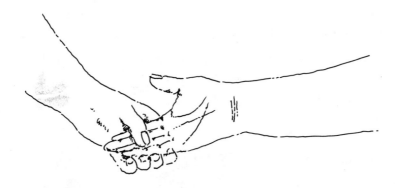

At one time having your hand read was taken very seriously. It was like going to a doctor. Today reading the hand is regarded more as fun, but it is just as interesting. One still studies the mounts, the tangle of lines, the Plain of Mars, and the rest of the geography that is supposed to tell what lies ahead.

Fortune-tellers say that your destiny is decided when you are born and is imprinted on your hands. However, the patterns on your two hands are not alike. Some lines are the same, but most are not. In fact, one hand may have lines that the other doesn't.

The hand to study is the one you use the most. If you are right-handed, study your right hand. Since you

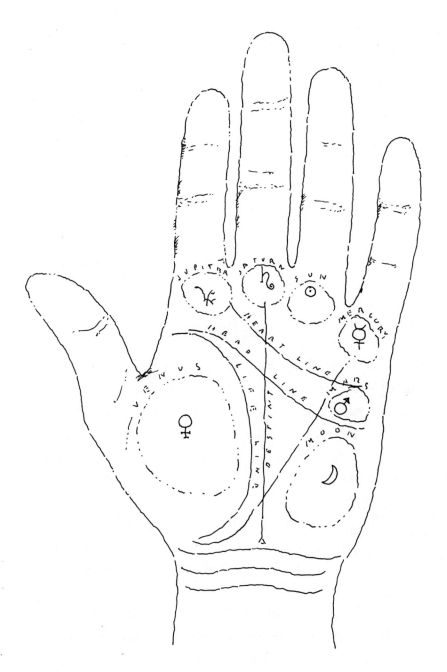

READING THE HAND

47

use it more, it may reflect your experiences more accurately than your left hand.

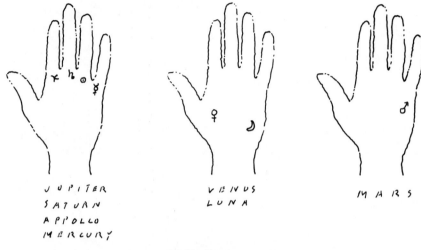

JUPITER
SATURN
APPOLLO
MERCURY

VENUS
LUNA

MARS

THE MOUNTS

These are the pads of flesh at the base of the thumb and each finger and around the outsides of the palm. Each mount is said to be a center for certain abilities and emotions, such as artistic abilities and love. A high, firm mount, for example, means that you are unusually artistic or loving. A low or flabby mount means the opposite.

There are seven mounts, each named for one of the heavenly bodies the first astrologers thought were gods. Here is where they are and what they are supposed to affect:

The base of the thumb: Mount of Venus, love

Below the first finger: Mount of Jupiter, ambition

Below the second finger: Mount of Saturn, independence

Below the third finger: Mount of the Sun, art

Below the little finger: Mount of Mercury, practical matters such as business

Below the Mount of Mercury: Mount of Mars, steadiness

Below the Mount of Mars: Mount of the Moon, imagination

THE LINES

There are countless creases, grooves, folds, and lines on our palms. Mark Twain called them a cobweb. The fortune-tellers say that only a few are important: the line of life, the heart line, the head line, and the line of destiny or fate. Each suggests what will happen over the course of a person's life. The early years are found where a line begins and the later years where it ends. A line will run from the top of the palm towards the bottom or from the inside towards the thumb.

In studying these lines, a fortune-teller examines their length, depth, and color. He looks for obstacles the lines cross and places at which a line breaks off and then continues.

A clear, even line means a simple, uncomplicated life.

A deeply cut line or one that is dark red suggests that strong emotions are involved.

Obstacles in the way of a line mean problems.

An X means illness or danger.

A series of dots suggests minor problems.

A cross-hatching of lines means complications.

A star or a triangle means good luck.

A break in a line means that a change of some kind will take place.

THE LINE OF LIFE. This line gives information about a person's health and how long he or she may live. It extends in a wide arc around the thumb.

A long, unbroken line means a long and healthy life. A short, unbroken line means a shorter, but healthy life.

A break in the line means a serious illness. If the line is broken towards the end, it means the person will not die until the age of eighty-five or so.

THE "M" LINE. Lines in the palm may form the letter M. The clearer the letter, the longer its owner is supposed to live.

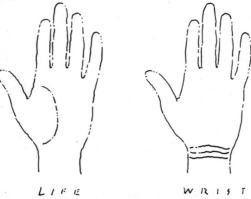

LIFE   WRIST

WRIST LINES. Often there are three horizontal lines on the underside of the wrist. If one is broken the person may not live to a great old age. If all the lines are clear and unbroken, happiness and riches lie ahead.

THE HEART LINE. This line tells how affectionate a person is. It reaches along the top of the palm, from under the little finger toward the first finger.

A clean, strong, unbroken line means a loving nature. If the line ends on the Mount of Jupiter, under the first finger, it means the person is very loving.

Each break in this line stands for a disappointment in love.

H E A R T

If the line resembles a chain, it means the person keeps changing his or her mind about whom he or she loves. If it has a tassel at one end, the person has too many close friends.

If the line runs through or near a circle, it means separation from a loved one for a while.

A triangle or a star nearby stands for good luck in love.

THE HEAD LINE. This line is concerned with a person's intelligence and interests. It extends across the center of the palm under the heart line.

A strong, clear head line means a strong, clear mind.

51

If the line moves straight across the palm, it means that the person is logical.

If the line curves down slightly, it suggests an interest in math or science.

If it curves down more sharply, it shows an interest in artistic things.

If the line reaches all the way down to the Mount of the Moon, the seat of the imagination, the person is unusually imaginative.

If the head line is close to the heart line, its owner is a cautious person.

If there is quite a bit of space between the two lines, it means the person is independent and high-spirited.

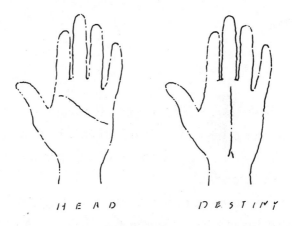

HEAD   DESTINY

THE LINE OF DESTINY OR FATE. This line may show what a person's career will be like over the years. It reaches from the Mount of Saturn under the second finger toward the wrist.

A long, unbroken line means quite a bit of success. But if another line crosses or there is a break in the line, it means a setback.

If the line fades away as it approaches the wrist, so will the person's career.

If the line ends in a small triangle near the wrist, it means a quiet, uneventful life.

Some people do not have a fate line. In others, it does not appear until they are adults.

THE PLAIN OF MARS

THE PLAIN OF MARS

This is the hollow of the hand. If the hollow is deep, some fortune-tellers say it means a timid person. If it is shallow, it means a confident person.

Other fortune-tellers look in the Plain of Mars for enemies a person may have. They rub the hollow with the ball of the thumb from the person's other hand. If there is an enemy nearby, doing so is said to cause his or her image to appear. The fortune-teller then mutters a curse, which protects the person, and the image fades.

— 8 —
Oracle Bones

Four thousand years ago, when the Chinese had questions about the future, they turned to their ancestors. And even though the ancestors were long dead, every ten days fortune-tellers sent them questions and received answers.

To send these questions, the Chinese fortune-tellers cut them into the surface of a turtle shell or the shoulder blade of an ox. "Should we conduct war against the barbarians?" the fortune-tellers once asked. "Will Lady Hao be in good health after she has her baby?" "Will [the king's] toothache cause [him] trouble?" "Will it rain tomorrow?"

For the answers, the fortune-tellers left a blank space

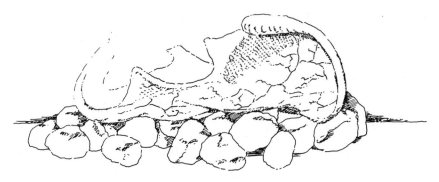

next to each question. Then, on the other side, under the blank space, they scraped away some of the shell or the bone. This weakened it so that it would crack when it was heated.

Then the fortune-tellers touched the blank space with a red-hot poker, there was a popping sound, and several cracks appeared. If two of the cracks formed an angle like this ⊢ , the answer to the question was yes. Otherwise, it was no.

Today this drawing, or ideograph, stands for the word "pu," which in Chinese means divination or fortune-telling. It is pronounced "bow!" like the popping sound when heat causes a bone or a shell to crack. Because they predicted the future, these bones became known in China as oracle bones.

In Labrador today the Naskapi Indians use a similar method in hunting the caribou. When the hunting is poor, the Naskapi heat the dried shoulder blade of a caribou over hot coals, which cracks the bone in several places. Then they use the cracks as a map to show where the hunting might be better. If they need meat badly, they make a new "map" every few days.

Scholars say that this method sometimes works. By chance the map points to areas where the Naskapi have not hunted before and where there will be caribou. Without this method they probably would return to the same hunting grounds where they had already killed much of the game.

The Naskapi do not know that this method of learning the future through oracle bones is one of the oldest on earth. Labrador is probably the only place where it still is used.

9
Dream Signs

Some dreams seem to foretell the future in startling ways. A person dreams that something is taking place, and later it does occur. A dream of Abraham Lincoln's is one of the most famous of such dreams.

In this dream President Lincoln saw himself walking from room to room in the White House. He could hear people crying softly, but he did not see anyone. When he walked into the East Room, he saw a coffin guarded by soldiers.

"Who is dead in the White House?" Lincoln asked the soldiers.

"The President," one of them said. "He was killed by an assassin."

A few days later Lincoln was shot and killed by John Wilkes Booth.

There are many such dreams. A woman whose husband worked in a silver mine in Colorado dreamed that high waves were pounding the cliffs in the village in England where she had once lived. When she awakened, she told her husband, "It is a bad omen," and convinced him not to go to work that day. "You might be killed," she said.

Later in the day one of his friends at the mine accidentally drilled through a wall into an abandoned mine shaft. The shaft filled with water that surged into the silver mine and drowned fourteen men. If it had not been for the woman's dream, fifteen men would have died.

The young son of a government official in Ireland came downstairs one morning saying, "I had such a nice dream. Somebody gave me a pretty box with my name on it." Taking a pencil, he drew the shape of a coffin. His mother and father stared at one another in alarm.

"Keep a close eye on him," the father begged his wife before leaving the house. But the boy slipped away and talked the coachman into giving him a ride. When the horse went out of control, the boy was thrown from the coach and killed.

In his children's book *Dreams*, the author Larry Kettelcamp describes a dream of his that came true. He dreamed he was walking along a highway. When he crossed a bridge, he saw an empty house. It was a ranch-style house, except that it had two floors at one end. In his dream, he tried to look inside through an upstairs window, but the window seemed to be covered by crossbars.

Two months later Mr. Kettelcamp and his family moved into a new house in another town. When he first saw the house, it looked vaguely familiar. Then he remembered his dream. It was the same house! The room he had tried to look into was the one he was going to use as his studio. What about the crossbars over the window? There weren't any, but the small panes of glass looked like bars. It was an empty house, as he had dreamed. The Kettelcamps were the first ones to live in it.

We may dream of the future more than we realize, and at times our dreams come true. One reason may be chance or coincidence. After all, we have five to ten dreams a night, or two thousand to three thousand dreams a year. With so many dreams, it is not surprising that a few predict what actually takes place.

Other dreams could come true because it is logical that they do so. Abraham Lincoln had every reason to be concerned that someone might kill him. At the end of the Civil War, there were many people who hated him.

With Mr. Kettelcamp's dream, he and his family were already planning to move. In his dream he crossed a bridge, which suggested making a fresh start. Undoubtedly, the family had talked about the kind of house they needed and hoped to find.

In ancient times people regarded dreams as omens of the future. Before Greek sailors went off on long voyages, they prayed to Poseidon, the god of the waters, to reveal in their dreams the problems they would face. Before generals, judges, and others began something important, they did the same with other gods.

In the past people who wanted to know what their dreams told about the future also went to fortune-tellers. Or they turned to dream books, or dictionaries of dreams. The most famous dream book was written two thousand years ago by a Roman named Artemidorus Daldianus. Since then thousands of such books have been published, and often they have been filled with nonsense.

We recall very few of our dreams, however, and often just bits and pieces of them. The methods listed below may help you to recall more of them. They will also help you learn how much you dream about the future and how accurate those dreams are.

1. When you awaken, don't look around; above all, don't look out the window. Concentrate on what you have been dreaming. The first thing you think of may be the subject of a dream you had.

2. Tell your dreams to someone. Doing so may help you to recall them. If you can't remember how a dream began, try to recall how it ended. Then work your way back toward the beginning. People once believed that telling a dream would make it come true.

3. Keep a notebook by your bed in which to write your dreams. Reread the dreams from time to time. You will learn how many were about the future and how many came true.

Even when we recall our dreams, it is hard to understand many of them. Some are simple enough, and we know what they are saying, but others are confusing. They seem to be in a secret language.

Here are some common subjects people dream about and the traditional meanings they have given them. Some are just the reverse of what you might expect.

If you dream of . . .	Its meaning is . . .
an accident	a happy surprise
animals: small animals	children
an ant	a reward for hard work
apes	secret enemies
a baby	bad news
a bald head	great riches

a basement	hidden fears, secret information
a basket	an invitation
a bat	unsuspected danger
a bear	disagreement with a friend
a running bear	happiness
a bridge	a fresh start
crossing a bridge	success at something important to you
a cat	treachery
a cauliflower	poverty; you may become poor and no one will take pity on you
a cemetery	news of death
chickens	bad luck
climbing down a hill	bad luck
climbing up a hill	good luck
clouds	a quarrel
a coffin	happiness
a cow	good fortune
a cradle	a wish that will come true
crying	unexpected happiness
a dandelion	treachery by a loved one
death: seeing a dead person; seeing yourself dead	long life in both cases
eating	illness
eggs: a great number of eggs	you are in love
broken eggs	trouble, death

falling	bad luck
a fire	anger and a quarrel
a house on fire	a death in your family
a fish	money
flowers	money
friends	enemies
funeral	wedding
gold	poverty
hair: having long hair when you have short hair or are bald	a change in your life
a horse: white horse	good luck
dark horse	disappointment
a journey	death
keys	someone is revealing secrets
a king	your father
kisses	deception
a letter	good luck
a lion	good luck

money	poverty
mud: you are up to your neck in mud	you will witness a crime, but not prevent it
music	sorrow
a queen	your mother
rats	treachery, enemies
a river: crossing a river	a turning point in your life
roses	you are falling in love
snakes	enemies
teeth: losing teeth	losing a friend, a death
a thief	trouble ahead
trees	joy, profit
a tunnel	danger
vegetables	well-behaved children
water: muddy water	trouble
clear water	good luck, good health

64

— 10 —
Death Signs

You hear a series of three knocking sounds at the front door, but when you go to the door, no one is there. Some say that these knocks are the sounds of nails being used to close a coffin—that they are warnings, or forerunners, that someone close to you is going to die.

A woman in Millinocket, Maine, said she had such an experience. We will call her Kate. For many years she had been friends with a woman named Helen. Kate and Helen promised that whoever died first would somehow let the other one know that she had died.

One evening Kate heard a knock at the door, but when she went to answer it, no one was there. Later in the evening she heard a second knock, but again no one was there. Finally, there was a third knock, and the same thing happened. Later that night, the telephone rang. It was Helen's son, Ted. He had called to tell Kate what she already knew—his mother had died.

Footsteps are a different kind of forerunner, like those that James Hardy, a sea captain, said he heard in his village in Nova Scotia. After an evening of visiting around a cozy stove with friends, he bundled up against the cold and started the long walk home. Soon he heard footsteps behind him. He stopped and turned to see who it was, but there was no one in sight. "Who is it?" he called. There was no answer, so he started walking again. Then he heard the footsteps once more and stopped. Again he heard and saw no one. But each time he resumed walking, he heard the footsteps behind him.

When James Hardy reached home, the footsteps stopped. His wife and sister were in the kitchen talking and asked him to join them, but he told his wife he wanted to speak to her privately.

"I am going to die tomorrow," he told her. But he looked so strong and well, she laughed. "Why do you say that?" she asked. "You look wonderful."

He told her about the footsteps. "I know it sounds ridiculous," he said, "but Death followed me all the way home."

She had heard such stories before, yet she could not believe it. "It is just one of those country superstitions," she said. "There is nothing to it." But her husband was so upset, she sat with him for a long time.

The next morning James Hardy got up as usual and went off to his ship, which was being overhauled. There was no point in staying home, he had told his wife. As he passed the ship, the stocks supporting it suddenly gave way, and the ship fell over and killed him.

Some people claim they have what is known as "second sight"—visions that enable them to see future events. Often these are visions of funerals that take place many weeks, or months, into the future. In such a vision, the person is walking along a road and feels himself or herself being pushed to one side. A hearse and a crowd of mourners go by. By identifying the mourners, the person knows who is in the coffin—and, therefore, who is going to die.

In Rockport, Maine, in the early 1900s, a girl of thirteen or fourteen had a similar vision. Her father had gone to Boston on business. According to the story, he came to the girl's room in a vision the second night he was away. He sat at the end of her bed and told her he was going to die. "Don't be frightened," he told her. "Just help take care of the family." Two days later they got word that he was dead.

In some country villages in England, people had a different way of learning when death would strike. According to legend, late at night on Saint Mark's Eve, April 24, a person standing on the porch of the local church would be able to see who would die in the year ahead. He or she would see their spirits pass by to enter the church.

One Saint Mark's Eve an old woman was said to have watched this parade of the doomed. She saw many faces she knew. When the last one of them turned and looked at her, she stared back. It was *her* spirit! She was staring at herself! She screamed and fainted. The next morning her neighbors found her on the porch of the church and took her home. She did not live long after that. The shock had been too great.

In some cases just a hunch is the warning about death. A person sees nothing and hears nothing to cause concern. But he or she senses that all is not right, that there is danger ahead, and tries to avoid it. This is called a premonition. Sometimes a person will not travel on an airplane or train or cross a bridge because of a premonition, and thus escapes death.

Some experts say these forerunners are based on imagination or coincidence. Others do not understand what is behind them. Predicting the future in this way is discussed in Chapter 12 and in the note to that chapter.

There are many other signs of death or danger in which people believe. If a picture suddenly falls from the wall, or a clock suddenly stops—or starts—or a bird pecks at the side of a house, it is such a sign. If a black beetle crawls up on your shoe, it also is one.

People have used other methods to learn when they will die:

When a clock strikes twelve at midnight on New Year's Eve, they enter a darkened room and look into a mirror. If they see what appears to be a coffin, they believe they will die in the year ahead.

A jump rope rhyme is supposed to tell you how much longer you have to live. The rhyme goes this way:

> *Apples, peaches, pumpkin pie,*
> *How many years before I die?*
> *One year, two years, three, four . . .*

Jump until you miss. It is said that the number you are reciting at the time will be the number of years you have remaining before you die.

11

Apollo and the Pythia

About twenty-five hundred years ago people in ancient Greece believed the gods would reveal the future to anyone who asked. They took their questions to temples and shrines throughout the country. The answers they received were called oracles.

The most famous temple was at Delphi on Mount Parnassus, where the god Apollo predicted what was to come. On the seventh day of all but the coldest months, all kinds of people went to Delphi: the rich, the poor, farmers, laborers, businessmen, even government officials. The questions they brought were about harvests, plagues, war, peace, personal business problems, and any other subject you might imagine.

Everyone brought an offering to Apollo. Usually it was a goat or a sheep to be sacrificed in his honor, but some brought gifts of gold, silver, and jewels. To have a question answered, each person also paid a fee that was equal to a half-day's income, or more.

When all those with questions had arrived, a priestess, usually a simple country woman, appeared. The Greeks believed that Apollo's spirit would occupy her body and speak through her mouth. The priestess was called the Pythia, after a dragon or serpent Apollo was supposed to have killed when he reached Delphi.

As the questioners watched, the Pythia would enter the inner sanctuary, seat herself on a stool of gold, and put herself into a trance.

When the Pythia's face and body turned red and began to swell, a priest asked the first question of Apollo. As he waited for an answer, the Pythia's head and body jerked violently. Her hair stood on end. She gasped for breath, frothed at the mouth, and made peculiar sounds. Then a flood of words poured out in a strange voice. The priest listened carefully, writing down what he could understand.

The priest asked a second question, then tried to write down another frenzy of words. He continued in this way until all the questions had been asked. As the Pythia left her trance, the priest wrote out the prophecies for each of the questioners.

Did Apollo really speak through the Pythia? Almost everyone in Greece believed that he did. The Pythia also believed it. Today we know this was not possible. But the Pythia believed it so strongly, scholars say, that she probably hypnotized herself into behaving as if it happened.

12

A Crystal Ball

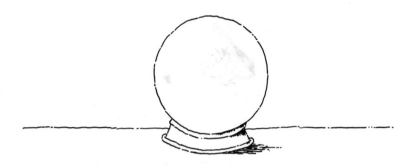

The soothsayer Jeane Dixon got her first crystal ball when she was eight years old. A fortune-teller who was a friend of her mother's gave it to her, for she sensed that the girl had the gift of prophecy. It is said that soon after Jeane received the crystal ball she began to see visions in it.

Over the years Jeane Dixon used a crystal ball to make many startling predictions, including the assassinations of President John F. Kennedy, his brother Robert F. Kennedy, and the black leader Martin Luther King, Jr.

When crystal balls came into use fifteen hundred years ago, they were condemned as the work of the

Devil. But they soon became as popular as astrology is today. You can still have your fortune told from a crystal ball. It is an eerie experience.

A crystal gazer works in a quiet, darkened room with his or her back to the light. The crystal ball is usually the size and shape of an orange or a hen's egg. The crystal gazer either keeps the ball in a holder on a table or holds it in the palm of the hand between the thumb and fingers. Some gazers shade the ball with a dark cloth to keep out any reflections. Others use the reflections to stimulate their minds and encourage visions.

When the fortune-teller is ready to begin, he empties his mind of all other thoughts and peers into the crystal ball, concentrating on a point deep inside. If the crystal becomes misty, it is a sign that the gazer soon will see something. If an image appears, he begins to predict the future.

This is what seemed to happen at a party Mamie Fish gave for her friends one summer day in Newport, Rhode Island. She had hired a fortune-teller with a crystal ball, and everyone at the party went to see him. Later they all had fun comparing what they had been told—all except for one young man named Vincent Walsh. "He couldn't see anything for me," Vincent told Mamie. "He stared and stared, then he said there was nothing to see."

When the party ended, Mamie told the crystal gazer how popular he had been. "Except for one person,"

she said. "He told me you didn't have anything for
him."

"A man of nineteen or twenty?"

Mamie nodded.

"You would not have wanted me to tell him what I
did see," the fortune-teller said. "I saw no future for
him because there is none to see. His life is finished.
He is going to die very soon."

Mamie looked at him in surprise.

"It is his destiny," he said. "I can't stop it. By this
time tomorrow he will be dead."

But when Mamie and a friend saw Vincent Walsh and his sister in a restaurant the next day, he was the picture of health. "It just shows," she whispered to her friend, "you shouldn't pay too much attention to fortune-tellers. He said 'by this time tomorrow.' That time has already passed, and Vincent is still alive."

Soon Vincent and his sister drove off with some friends. An hour later a man came into the restaurant white-faced and shaking. "There has been a dreadful accident," he said. "Vincent Walsh is dead."

Had the prophecy come true? That's a question we will return to later in this chapter.

How does an image get into a crystal ball? Fortune-tellers say the image forms in their minds and then they project it into the crystal. How this is possible is not understood, but that is what they say.

If you want to try crystal gazing, a crystal ball is not essential. Any surface in which you can see an image will do: a hand mirror, a piece of polished metal, a basin of water, or even a thumbnail lightly coated with oil. In Egypt a pool of black ink held in the palm of a hand has been used. Experts say you also will need a quiet, semidark room.

First, stare into the shiny surface for a half hour or more. Concentrate. If you don't see anything, the experts suggest you try several times over a period of a few weeks before you give up. Then try again at a later date. They say that the ability to see visions in a crystal ball may be present only at certain times.

In the Middle Ages people believed that only someone who had not committed any sins could see visions in a crystal. That is why a fortune-teller would hire a boy or girl to serve as his eyes whenever he could not see anything. Such a person was called a scryer. He or she would get under a blanket and stare into a hand mirror, trying to see an image that would help predict the future.

Crystal gazing also was used to track down thieves or stolen goods or persons who were missing. For a fee, a fortune-teller would search for them in his crystal.

In 1761 in a small English village two men went to see a fortune-teller named Jonathan Crowther. They wanted him to find a neighbor who had been missing for twenty days. The fortune-teller told them to bring back a boy of twelve or thirteen to help him. The men returned with Jonas Rushford, who later told this story to the famous minister John Wesley.

"When we came in, he put me into a bed, with a looking glass in my hand, and covered me with a blanket. Then he asked me whom I had a mind to see, and I said, 'My mother.' Directly, a light seemed to break out in the glass. Presently I saw her standing with a lock of wool in her hand. Later she told me she was standing just where I saw her and in the same clothes.

"Then he bid me look again for the man that was missing, who was one of our neighbors. I looked and saw him riding on a horse, but he was very drunk, and he stopped at the alehouse and drank two pints more. And he pulled out some money to change.

"I saw two men there, a big man and a little man, and when he pulled out the money, I saw them leave before he did. . . . When he came up to the top of a hill, they pulled him off his horse and killed him. Then they took his money and threw him into a coal pit. If I saw them again, I would know them.

"The next day I went with our neighbors and showed them the spot where he was killed, and the pit where he was thrown. A man went down and brought him up. It was just as I told them. . . ."

Whether Jonas actually saw this or only remembered it this way is, of course, something we do not know.

Some people were convinced that Mrs. Dixon could see into the future. If so, how could that be? And what about those who seem to see the future in their dreams or in some other way? It is something we don't understand as yet, but there are many theories about what might be involved.

According to one theory, there are times when a person is most likely to let go of the present and see something of what lies ahead. This might be when he or she is very tired, or very relaxed, or has been dreaming. It also might happen when someone empties his mind of the present and concentrates on the future, as a crystal gazer tries to do.

Another of these theories has to do with time. Some persons regard time as a kind of path we follow through life. From this path we see the present and can look back to the past, but we can't see into the future. A few suggest that there may be another path, parallel to the first, along which our unconscious travels. This is the path we take, they say, if we have visions of what lies ahead.

These ideas suggest that the future already exists or already has been planned in some way. However, many people believe that the future occurs only when it happens. The best way to predict the future, they say, is to understand what is going on today and what may happen as a result.

— 13 —

Your Future in an Egg

Two hundred years ago young people in America and England used the following method to learn what the future might hold for them.

Fill a jar with cold water three quarters of the way to the top. With a pin make a small hole in the bottom of an uncooked egg and another at the top. Let three or four drops of egg white fall into the water. Then wait and watch. During the next several hours the egg white will slowly spread through the jar, forming lovely, mysterious shapes.

If you see a flower, it means you will not marry for at least another year. A ring or a church steeple means that you will marry within the year.

You may see a star, which means you will be healthy all year long. A coffin means just the opposite.

If you see a ship, a sail, or an anchor in the jar, you will take a journey or become a sailor or marry one.

Tall buildings mean you will visit a big city, or work or live in one. Furrowed fields mean life on a farm.

In years gone by the jar was placed in front of a fire or candle to better reveal the shapes forming inside. Today a flashlight also can be used.

— 14 —
Astrology

Astrologers believe that the sun, moon, and five planets that can be seen with the naked eye have an influence on your future. This idea goes back four thousand years to ancient Babylonia, where astrology was first used.

In much of the world today astrology still is the most popular means of telling fortunes. In the United States, six teenagers out of ten are said to believe in astrology.

Each day throughout the world, millions upon millions of people read their horoscopes in newspapers, magazines, and almanacs to learn what the day may bring and how to deal with it. Many of them also have horoscopes prepared that spell out what they can expect in the years ahead.

Other people turn to astrologers for advice—on whom to marry, when to have a child, whether or not to make a business deal or take a trip or buy a house, and any other important decision. The astrologer studies the positions of the sun, the moon, and the planets, then, based on that, advises them what to do.

Some governments have been known to use astrology to help reach decisions. During the Second World War Adolf Hitler relied on astrologers to advise him on strategy. But when the astrologers predicted his defeat, Hitler had them locked away in concentration camps. Meanwhile, the English had hired their own astrologer to learn what advice Hitler was getting.

Astrology is important in the modern world. Yet there are many people, including leading scientists, who think it is pure nonsense. Let's explore how astrology is supposed to work.

YOUR ASTROLOGICAL SIGN

Your birthdate reveals the astrological sign under which you were born—whether you are, for example, an Aries or a Taurus. And that tells a believer in astrology quite a lot about you. The signs, and characteristics that are said to go with them, are listed according to the astrological year.

 ARIES, THE RAM, MARCH 21—APRIL 19.

You are lively, adventurous, funny, and full of ideas.
You make friends easily, and your friends turn to you
to lead them. But you are impatient and stubborn, and
tend to be irritable when you don't get your way.

 TAURUS, THE BULL, APRIL 20—MAY 20.

You are an artistic person. You also are a hard worker,
and you depend on yourself, not on others. You are
practical and patient and you usually are easy to get
along with. But you can be as stubborn and determined
as a bull. It takes a while for you to get angry, but if
someone does anger you, they had better watch out.

 GEMINI, THE TWINS, MAY 21—JUNE 20.

You are a cheerful, lively, changeable person. Often
you don't finish what you start. You have a tendency
to pass up good opportunities. You may readily give up

one friend for another, or a job or a sport in which you could be outstanding if only you stuck to it.

CANCER, THE CRAB, JUNE 21—JULY 22.
You are a very private person. You tend to be secretive and hard to know, like a crab. You are like a crab in another way. Once you get hold of something, you hang on to it. Your room is filled with things you don't need but won't throw away.

LEO, THE LION, JULY 23—AUGUST 22.
In some ways you are quite a bit like a lion. You are determined and brave and loyal and affectionate. At times you are also bossy, and become angry and roar when someone disagrees with you.

VIRGO, THE VIRGIN, AUGUST 23—SEPTEMBER 23.
You love reading and thinking about things. You have

opinions about almost everything and you freely express them. Some believe you tend to be too critical; now and then they may be right.

♎ LIBRA, THE SCALES, SEPTEMBER 24–OCTOBER 21.
You tend to balance everything very carefully, like a set of scales, before reaching a decision. You want to be fair and are sympathetic and understanding. As a result, you are slow to make up your mind or take sides in an argument.

♏ SCORPIO, THE SCORPION, OCTOBER 22–NOVEMBER 21.
You are at your best when making and carrying out decisions. You are at your worst when you let your emotions take over. But usually you are thoughtful and quiet.

♐ SAGITTARIUS, THE ARCHER, NOVEMBER 22–DECEMBER 21.

You like being with people and make friends easily. But you tend to say whatever is on your mind. At times you hurt someone's feelings without meaning to. You love sports like archery in which you can compete against yourself or just a few other persons.

CAPRICORN, THE GOAT, DECEMBER 22–JANUARY 20.
You are a serious, ambitious person. You don't like fooling around and wasting time. You work at things with patience and care, and are good at meeting challenges and overcoming obstacles.

AQUARIUS, THE WATER BEARER, JANUARY 21–FEBRUARY 19.
You are for brotherhood and equality. You believe that everyone is special, that there is no such thing as an ordinary person. You also believe that everyone should do his own thing, as long as no one suffers. You are intelligent, artistic, generous, and friendly, yet you are unpredictable. Often no one knows what you are going to do next, except that it will be interesting.

PISCES, THE FISHES, FEBRUARY 20—MARCH 20.
You are a gentle, cautious, dreamy person, but you also
are moody and changeable. One minute you may be
as lively as can be and the next as quiet as can be. You
love artistic things, and, just as fish do, you love the
water.

SEVEN GODS

The first astrologers were priests in Babylonia, in
what today is the Middle East. The Babylonians believed that gods controlled everything that happened
to them. The most powerful were seven gods they could
see in the sky with their own eyes—Sun, Moon, Venus,
Mercury, Mars, Saturn, and Jupiter.

Day after day these gods moved around the earth in
an unending procession. They seemed so close, the
astrologers decided the earth must be at the very center
of the heavens. Since these were considered such powerful gods, the astrologers believed they controlled the
future of every person on earth.

By keeping a close watch on where these gods were
and what they were doing, they believed, one could
learn what the future would bring. The astrologers of

Babylonia did this by preparing sky charts, or maps of the sky.

If two planets came together at the same time that a crop failed or a battle was lost, the astrologers blamed the gods. When they saw the two planets in the same position in the future, they expected trouble again. In this way the Babylonian sky charts began to serve as horoscopes.

What is remarkable about astrology is how it survived, grew, and spread. By the sixteenth century, thousands of years after it began, a vast number of people still believed that astrology could solve their problems. Astrology was regarded as a science. It was studied at universities and astrologers were among the most learned and respected people of their time.

Many astrologers had private practices, just as doctors and lawyers do today. An astrologer would cast a horoscope for the precise time a person was born that would tell what kind of life he or she could expect to lead. Then once each year the astrologer would predict in detail what the year ahead would be like. Whenever a person had special questions, he would also answer them, such as whether to get married, when someone would die, or even where a treasure was buried.

A part of an astrologer's work had nothing to do with the future, but suggested how important astrology had become. People came to astrologers for advice on personal problems. Some astrologers even practiced medicine, but in a most curious way. They told what made a person sick and what would cure him or her based on a study of heavenly signs.

Then the idea on which astrology was based was challenged. For thousands of years astrologers had said that the earth was at the center of the universe. The stars and the planets moved around the earth and determined a person's future.

But when the telescope was invented in the seventeenth century, scientists learned that the universe was not like the one that astrologers had described. The earth was not at the center. It was just a tiny speck in a vast sea of heavenly bodies, many of which could not even be seen with the naked eye. The scientists concluded that astrology was based not on fact, but on traditional beliefs that were not correct.

Astrology was no longer regarded as a learned science. Universities stopped the study of it. But to most people, none of this mattered. They continued to visit astrologers to have their horoscopes cast and to learn the future, just as people do today.

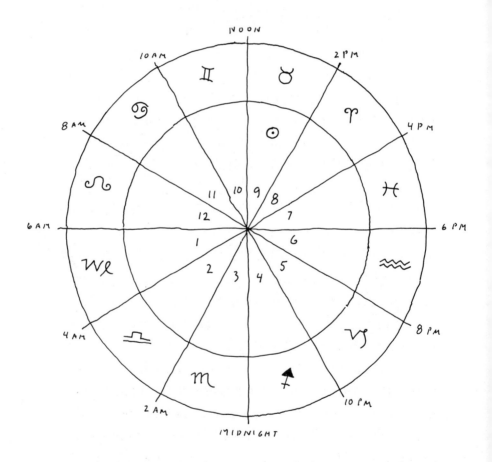

CASTING A HOROSCOPE

Modern astrologers say that the horoscopes one reads in a newspaper or a magazine may be fun, but they are worthless. What you should do, they claim, is have a horoscope cast especially for yourself.

You can take many of the steps an astrologer takes in casting such a horoscope. You will need your date of birth, the time you were born within fifiteen minutes, and your place of birth.

1. Draw a circle about five inches in diameter. Inside draw a smaller circle about four inches in diameter.

2. Draw a horizontal line across the center of both circles. It stands for the horizon. Then draw a vertical line through the center. Write "noon" at the top of the vertical line and "midnight" at the bottom.

3. Divide each of the four parts of the circles into thirds, as shown in the drawing on page 92. Moving clockwise from noon, mark the time at two-hour intervals, starting with two o'clock, then four o'clock, and so on.

Each of these parts is a "house" that regulates one part of your life. House 1 affects your personality; house 2, money; 3, education and knowledge; 4, home; 5, children; 6, friendship; 7, love and marriage; 8, death; 9, journeys; 10, jobs; 11, goals; 12, illness, disgrace, and other problems.

4. Check the list of birthdates earlier in this chapter for your astrological sign.

5. Locate the part of the circle that contains the time of day when you were born. In it draw the symbol for the sun, which is a circle with a dot in it. Draw your astrological sign on the outside edge of the section. In our drawing, we have used the sign for Taurus.

6. Moving counterclockwise, or opposite from the way the clock moves, draw the eleven remaining astrological signs, one in each house. The order backwards from Taurus is Gemini, Cancer, Leo, Virgo, Libra, Scorpio, Sagittarius, Capricorn, Aquarius, Pisces, and Aries.

7. Find the 4 A.M. to 6 A.M. section. The sign you have written in that house was rising on the horizon the day you were born. It is called your "ascendant." This is an important sign in casting a horoscope. Number the houses 1 to 12, moving counterclockwise from this house.

This is about as far as you can go on your own. At this point an astrologer turns to an ephemeris—a book of tables that gives the positions of the planets, the sun, the moon, comets, and other bodies at the time you were born. He or she enters these positions on your horoscope, then decides how the stars will affect your life.

Were there two planets side by side? Were there two separated by 60 degrees (a good omen), or by 90 degrees (a bad omen), or by 120 degrees (a very good omen)? Or was one planet opposite another (a bad omen)?

Also, how did the planets, other bodies, and astrological signs affect the houses when you were born? Since each house is supposed to affect a different aspect of your life, this is very important.

If the Moon was in house 2 when you were born, it could be the reason you are wasteful and spend more money than you should. If the planet Mercury was in house 7 at the time, it could be the reason you work well with others. If the Sun was in house 9, it may mean that someday you will receive unexpected money and use it for a long journey.

Little has changed. How astrologers decide what lies ahead is not very different from the way Babylonian priests peered into the heavens four thousand years ago in their search for the future. And a great many people still look to the stars for what is to come.

Telling Fortunes—and Magic

Telling fortunes has more to do with magic than with anything else. Through a kind of magic people who use astrology give stars and planets the power to affect their lives, when actually a star or a planet does not have this power. It is the same kind of magic power people give to omens, tea leaves, playing cards, and other things they use to tell the future.

People often use these methods when there is no other way of learning what they want to know. Yet the answers they get can be misleading.

There is one way these ancient methods of predicting the future can be helpful. As I wrote at the beginning of this book, they start us thinking about the many possibilities that lie ahead for us. They also can be fun—if we don't take them too seriously. When we do, we rely on magic.

A.S.

Notes,
Sources,
and
Bibliography

Notes

The publications cited are described in the Bibliography.

Birthdays (Chapter 1). In several versions of this nineteenth century nursery rhyme, some surprising children are described. In one, Thursday's child "is inclined to thieving." In another, Friday's child is "full of sin." But in every version Sunday's child is always blessed. He or she is "bonny and blithe," and "never shall want" and "to Heaven [their] steps shall tend always." Opie, *Dictionary*, pp. 311–12.

Ditches, Holes, Dirt, and Nails (Chapter 1). Although mothers and fathers are frequently at risk, in some places so are grandmothers and the Devil. But in only one instance is a child threatened. That is in the A. A. Milne poem "Lines and Squares." If the young boy steps on a line, he will be chased by a bear. "And the little bears growl to each other, 'He's mine, / as soon as he's silly and steps on a line.' " See Milne, pp. 14–15.

For other chapters with omens see "Love Magic," Chapter 2; "Dream Signs," Chapter 9; and "Death Signs," Chapter 10. See the Note "Apollo and the Pythia" to Chapter 11. For a book of omens, see Schwartz, *Cross Your Fingers.*

Omens and augurs (Chapter 1). There have been experts on omens throughout much of history. The most famous were the augurs in the days of the Roman Empire two thousand years ago.

An augur's job was to learn whether the gods approved of what someone planned to do. Was it all right, for example, for a man to marry a certain woman or buy a business or take a trip?

The Roman government also was worried about how the gods felt. If it made war on another country, would the gods object and bring ruin upon Rome? Only an augur could tell for sure.

The advice an augur gave depended on the omens he saw. With a long, crooked staff, he marked out a section of the sky or a part of the countryside where he expected to see a sign from the gods. Then he settled down to watch for one.

The sign might have been a flash of lightning, the sound of thunder, or even a flight of birds. The augur studied the direction from which the birds came, how high they were flying, and the sounds they made, and he decided what all of this meant.

At other times the augur watched for other signs. If someone sneezed or stumbled, or if a chair creaked, that had special meaning. Sometimes he also sacrificed an animal to a god and examined the liver and other organs. If their size, shape, or color was not normal or if they had strange marks on them, these were omens to consider.

Love magic (Chapter 2). Countless techniques have been devised to learn what lies ahead when it comes to love and marriage. Most are originally from the eighteenth and nineteenth centuries. A number are pure foolery, but many are

102

serious efforts. They suggest what a desolate life awaited those who failed to marry and had to remain at home or live alone.

"*One, I love*" (Chapter 2). There are many versions of this rhyme. Along with those in the text, try "He loves me, longs for me, desires me, wishes me well, wishes me ill, does not care," and, in French, "*Elle m'aime un peu, beaucoup, passionnément, pas du tout.*" Opie, *Dictionary*, p. 332.

"*What will life be like. . .*" (Chapter 2). A similar method of fortune-telling, with some important differences, is used at a girls' school in Pittsburgh. It is called "MASH," which stands for "Mansion, Apartment, Shack, House." As in the text, a girl draws a large rectangle, but at the top she writes MASH. To the left she lists the names of four boys she likes. To the right she writes four numbers, which tell the number of children she may have. At the bottom she lists the names of four places she might live when she is married.

The girl places the point of a pencil in the center of the box, closes her eyes, and moves the pencil around and around in an ever-enlarging circle like the trail of a snail until she is told to stop. The result looks like this:

Next the girl counts the number of circular lines she has made. Starting with the letters M-A-S-H, she counts through the items in each of the lists, stopping when she reaches that number. She crosses out that item, then repeats the process until there is only one item left in each of the four lists. Jamie Kahn, 10, Winchester-Thurston School, Pittsburgh, 1983.

Yes or no (Chapter 3). In the Old Testament it is said that Hebrew priests used the "yes-no" method of divination each time they wished to learn what God wanted them to do. Instead of slips of paper, they chose from two pieces of stone, bone, or wood, one marked with *Urim* for yes, the other with *Thummin* for no. Exodus 28:30.

Arab priests in Mecca later used a quiver from which they drew one of three arrows to guide their actions. On one was written "My Lord hath forbidden me"; on another, "My Lord hath commanded me." The third arrow was blank. Jones, p. 262.

At Pharae in ancient Greece, the "words in a crowd" method included a statue of the god Hermes. Someone with a question about the future would whisper it into the statue's ear, then hurry off to a busy street. The first words he overheard were his answer. "Oracle," p. 1018.

For other ways in which lots are used in divination, see "Love Magic," Chapter 2, in which the alphabet is recited, daisy petals are plucked, and slips of paper are drawn from under a pillow, among other methods. Also see "Oracle Bones," Chapter 8.

Lots also have been used to decide who is "it" in a game, settle disputes, decide a course of action, divide property, decide who is guilty, and select officials. Of course, they also are the basis of gambling.

Oracle bones (Chapter 8). The use of oracle bones is mentioned in accounts of early Chinese history. This method was all but forgotten, however, until a strange discovery in 1899 by a Chinese scholar who was ill. The scholar's name was Wang, and his field of study was words. His doctor had prescribed "dragon bones," an old Chinese folk remedy that is rich in calcium. It consists of pulverized bone, including bits and pieces of ancient animal bones. Wang was startled to find that some were inscribed with a very early form of Chinese writing from the oracle bones of old. Chou, p. 135.

Dream signs and dream cures (Chapter 9). The questions ancient people took to the temples included pleas for advice on how to cure their illnesses and handicaps. They, too, slept where they prayed, hoping a god would speak to them in their dreams.

In Japan the story is told of a girl who was unable to speak because her tongue was too short. Her nurse brought her to a temple in search of a cure. After they prayed, they spent the night there, and the girl and her nurse had the same dream. A priest said to them, "In an honest and noble face, the tongue should always reach the end of the nose." He then stretched the girl's tongue until it reached the tip of her nose. And in the morning, when the girl awakened, she was able to speak.

In Greece a person who was ill prayed to Asclepius, the god of healing. According to legend, a man with an ugly red mark on his forehead dreamed that the god had wrapped a bandage around his head. When he awakened both the bandage and the mark were gone.

Some believe that these dreams helped a person overcome a psychological problem, which in turn helped start a cure. What occurred was recorded in writing on the wall of the temple or inscribed on a plaque placed on a stone column where others could read about it.

It was said that Hippocrates, the early Greek physician regarded as the father of medicine, learned some of what he knew from the dream cures described at the temple of Asclepius in Cos, where he lived. Loewe, pp. 75, 76, Seligmann, p. 50.

Apollo and the Pythia (Chapter 11). According to legend, the Pythia went into a trance by breathing a vapor that escaped from a crevice in the stone under her gold stool. But geologists have found that the underlying rock could not have produced a vapor of any kind. It is likely that she did enter a trance, as noted in the text. "Oracle," p. 1016.

The god Apollo was one of a family of twelve Olympian gods and goddesses who, according to myth, lived in the remote Olympia mountain range of northern Greece.

Apollo's father was Zeus, the supreme Greek god, and his mother was the fertility goddess Hera. His uncle Hades was the lord of the underworld, and his uncle Poseidon was the lord of the waters. In addition, Apollo had scores of lesser relatives.

These gods looked and behaved like humans. Unlike gods elsewhere, they were not all-powerful, but they did live forever and were able to predict the future.

Zeus offered his prophecies at a temple in Dodona in

northwest Greece, the first center of prophecy in the region. He used omens to tell the future rather than utterance as Apollo did. The ways in which the leaves in a sacred oak tree rustled were construed as answers to questions about the future, as were the clangings of metal vases hung in the tree and the cooing of doves that rested there. A sacred spring at Dodona also told the future based on movements of leaves and other objects dropped in the water.

There also were centers of prophecy in Libya, Egypt, Turkey, Syria, Rome, and other countries.

A crystal ball (Chapter 12). The belief in clairvoyance, telepathy, and precognition has roots in the psychical research movement of the nineteenth century and earlier, which also was concerned with the idea of life after death. Today this field is called parapsychology. It includes experimentation in extrasensory perception (ESP), which takes in perceptions beyond the normal range, and psychokinesis (PK), in which movements of an object are affected by thoughts about it.

Research in parapsychology has not been taken seriously by scientists. One reason is that there is little understanding of what lies behind these phenomena, whether they exist, and how they work. Another is that it has not been possible to readily repeat experiments in parapsychology since they involve abnormal situations that may occur at one time but not at another.

The prophecies of the psychic Jeane Dixon have no scientific explanation, although parapsychologists believe that they result from a form of precognition. Various sources.

Attitudes of teenagers toward ESP and astrology (Chapters

107

12, 14). In a 1984 Gallup Youth Survey of 502 young people in the United States, fifty-nine percent of teenagers between thirteen and eighteen said they believed in ESP. Fifty-five percent said they believed in astrology.

Telling fortunes—and magic (Afterword). The magic used in divination is imitative magic in which one thing affects another because it is similar in some way. A break in the life line of the palm suggests serious illness or death, for example. Or two heavenly bodies that seem in conflict to an astrologer may foretell a conflict in a person's life.

Abbreviations in Sources and Bibliography

AA	*American Anthropologist*
CFQ	*California Folklore Quarterly*
FCB	*The Frank C. Brown Collection of North Carolina Folklore*
IUFA	Indiana University Folklore Archive, Bloomington
JAF	*Journal of American Folklore*
MAFS	Memoirs of the American Folklore Society
NEFA	Northeast Archives of Folklore and Oral History, University of Maine, Orono
RU	Compiler's collection of folklore from his students at Rutgers University, 1963–78
UPFA	University of Pennsylvania Folklore Archive
WF	*Western Folklore*

Sources

The sources of each item are given, along with variants and related information. When available, the names of collectors (C) and informants (I) are given. The publications cited are described in the Bibliography.

Epigraph

p. iii   *Rich man, poor man.* Oral tradition.

What Is Going to Happen?

p. 7   *Spinning a knife.* Author's childhood experience, Brooklyn, N.Y., 1940s; Addy, p. 82, England. A bottle is used as a spinner, *FCB* 5858, North Carolina.

1   Omens

pp. 10–13   *Beds.* Compiler's childhood recollection, Brooklyn, N.Y., 1940s; Thomas, *Religion*, p. 623, England; *Bees.* MacKay, p. 299; Addy, p. 65, England; *Beetles.* RU, 1975, New Jersey; Opie, *Lore*, p. 213, England; *Birthdays.* Opie, *Dictionary*, p. 312, England.

     Cats. Oral tradition; *Ditches, holes, dirt, and*

nails. Oral tradition; *Dogs.* MacKay, p. 299; *Ears.* FCB 4086–88, North Carolina; Opie, *Lore,* p. 328; *Flowers.* RU, 1975; *Funerals.* Compiler's childhood recollection, 1940s; *Hairs.* Addy, p. 86, England; *Hands.* Roberts, *JAF* 40, #116, Louisiana; compiler's childhood recollection, 1940s; *Horses.* FCB 7100.

Knives. Oral tradition; *Ladders.* RU, 1975; *Ladybugs.* Oral tradition; *Moon.* FCB 653; *Noses.* MacKay, p. 299; *Pigs.* MacKay, p. 298, given as sow; *Shoelace.* RU, 1975; *Sneezing.* Various sources; *Socks.* RU, 1968; MacKay, p. 299; *Spiders.* FCB 3992, 3998; rhyme, oral tradition; *Wrists.* Addy, p. 95.

2   Love Magic

p. 14   *Apple.* Oral tradition.

p. 15   *Ice cream soda.* Oral tradition.

p. 15   *He loves me / he don't.* Botkin, *Folksay,* p. 164.

pp. 15–16 *A ring on a hair.* Gardner, p. 275, Schoharie County, N.Y.; Henderson, pp. 106–7, Jones, p. 198, both England.

p. 16   *Slips of paper.* FCB 4841, North Carolina.

pp. 16–17 *One, I love.* Hyatt 6781, Illinois; FCB 4182, 4183, 4591, 4592, North Carolina; Opie, *Lore,* p. 336, England. See the Note "One, I love" (Chapter 2).

pp. 17–18 *Matching names.* Creighton, *Magic,* p. 183, Nova Scotia; Hand, *Compendium,* 13011–13, Ohio.

p. 18   *The new moon.* Randolph, *Magic,* pp. 174–75, Missouri.

111

pp. 18–19   *Dumb supper.* Randolph, *Magic*, pp. 178–81; Hand, *Compendium*, 13085–89, Ohio.

p. 19   *Bend your thumb.* Compiler's childhood recollection, Brooklyn, N.Y., 1940s.

p. 20   *Dandelion seeds.* Oral tradition.

p. 20   *Big toe.* FCB 4626.

p. 21   *How many children?* Daisy seeds, Gardner, p. 276; apple seeds, forehead wrinkles, oral tradition; pinkie wrinkles, Maurice Hawk School, West Windsor, N.J., 1983; flat stone, Randolph, *Magic*, p. 186.

p. 22   *A large rectangle.* Oral tradition. For MASH, a variant, see the Note "What will life be like . . ." (Chapter 2).

p. 23   *Matching names.* Hyatt, 13016.

3   Yes or No?

p. 24   *Yes or no.* Hand, *Compendium*, 25131, Ohio; Ellis, pp. 49–51.

p. 25   *A word.* Compiler's childhood recollection, Brooklyn, N.Y., 1940s.

p. 25   *A hair comb.* Whitney 1593, Maryland.

p. 25   *A pebble. Encyclopedia of Superstition*, pp. 28–81.

p. 25   *A page in a book.* Jones, p. 221; Hand, *Compendium*, 24828–33; FCB 3489–91, 5849, North Carolina.

p. 25   *Words in a crowd.* Jones, p. 222; "Oracle," p. 1018.

p. 26   *Three dice.* Bowness, pp. 83–84, Gypsy culture; Hyatt 9057, Illinois.

p. 27   *Mashed potatoes.* Opie, *Lore*, pp. 273–74, Eng-
             land; Hand, *Compendium*, 25141–43.

4   Reading Tea Leaves

pp. 28–29   *Tea leaf ritual.* Bowness, pp. 86–87, Gypsy cul-
            ture; FCB 5859, North Carolina; Hand, *Com-
            pendium*, 25145, Ohio; Bei, general.
pp. 30–31   *Tea leaf shapes.* Hand, *Compendium*, FCB;
            Whitney; Hyatt, Illinois; Bei; Bowness; Opie,
            Lore, p. 340, England; Johnson, p. 19, New
            England.
p. 32   *Bubbles.* FCB 3429, 3430; Whitney 1583, 1584,
            Maryland.

5   A Cootie Catcher

IUFA, (I) Mollie Kramer, 11, Forest, Ind., (C) Carolyn
Kramer, 1970; Barbara Carmer Schwartz, childhood recollection, Delmar, N.Y., 1940s. See Knapp, pp. 257–58;
Opie, *Lore*, pp. 341–42, a film star oracle with which names
of movie stars and flowers are used instead of colors and
numbers, England.

6   Reading the Cards

pp. 38–39   *Yes or no.* Knapp, p. 259.
p. 39   *A marriage card.* Author's childhood recollec-
            tion, Brooklyn, N.Y., 1940s.
pp. 40–41   *Nine cards.* Hyatt, 9054, Illinois; Hand, *Com-
            pendium*, 25179, Ohio; Ellis, pp. 60–61, Eng-
            land.

pp. 41–43   *Hearts, diamonds, clubs, spades.* Bowness, pp. 78–83, Gypsy culture; Hand, *Compendium*, 4834, 6490, 6618, 20405, 20578, 27698, 27699; Thomas, *Kentucky*, p. 249, Kentucky.

p. 43   *Special meanings.* Hand, *Compendium*, 13377–81, 20577, 25176–77.

pp. 44–45   *Tarot.* Seligmann, pp. 271–85.

7   Reading the Hand

General. Bowness, pp. 65–72, Gypsy culture; Ellis, pp. 62–67, England; Henderson, pp. 107–9, England; Seligmann, pp. 266–71; Thomas, *Religion*, p. 631; Thomson, pp. 40–53.

pp. 49–50   *Obstacles, stars.* FCB 5854, North Carolina; Gibson, pp. 304–5.

p. 50   *Line of life.* FCB 667, 5851, 5852, 6620.

p. 50   *"M" line.* FCB 666; Hyatt 3329, Illinois.

p. 50   *Wrist lines.* FCB 5853.

p. 53   *Plain of Mars.* Bowness, p. 65.

8   Oracle Bones

In China, Chou, pp. 134–39; Loewe, pp. 43–46; in Labrador, Moore, pp. 69–74.

9   Dream Signs

pp. 57–58   *Lincoln's death dream.* Traditional legend.

p. 58   *Silver mine.* Bancroft, pp. 324–25, Colorado.

pp. 58–59   *The young son.* Henderson, p. 340, England.

pp. 59–60   *Kettelcamp's Dream.* Kettelcamp, *Dream*, P. 78.

p. 60　　　　*Dreams in ancient Greece.* Seligmann, pp. 49–51.

pp. 61–64　*Dream signs: Accident,* traditional; *animals,* compiler; *ant,* Bowness, p. 74, Gypsy culture; *apes,* Weiss, p. 523; *baby,* traditional; *bald head,* RU, 1968; *basement, basket, bat,* traditional; *bear, bridge,* Bowness, p. 74; *crossing a bridge,* traditional.

Cat, traditional; *cauliflower,* MacKay, p. 293; *cemetery,* traditional; *chickens,* Randolph, *Magic,* p. 330, Missouri; *climbing a hill,* FCB 3743, North Carolina; *clouds,* traditional; *coffin, cow, cradle,* Bowness, p. 75; *crying,* traditional; *dandelion,* Kell, p. 370; *death,* Hand, *Compendium,* 6493, 6494; FCB 4392.

Eating, traditional; *eggs,* FCB 3363, 4488; Johnson, p. 23, New England; *falling,* Johnson, p. 20; *fire,* FCB 3542; Johnson, p. 22; Whitney 707, Maryland; *fish,* Sackett 2844, Kansas; traditional; *flowers, friends,* traditional; *funeral,* FCB 4392; *gold,* traditional.

Hair, Smiley, p. 381, South; *horse,* Bowness, p. 76; *journey,* traditional; *keys,* Creighton, *Magic,* p. 114, Nova Scotia; *king,* traditional; *kisses,* traditional; *letter,* RU, 1968; *lion,* compiler; *money, mud,* MacKay, p. 293; *music,* compiler; *queen,* traditional.

Rats, FCB 3609; *river, roses,* traditional; *snakes,* Johnson, p. 22; Whitney 677; Randolph, *Magic,* p. 330; *teeth,* traditional; *thief,* Bowness, p. 78; *trees,* Saxon, p. 123; *tunnel,* Bowness, p. 78;

vegetables, RU, 1968; *water*, Randolph, *Magic*, p. 330; FCB 3108; Creighton, *Magic*, p. 113.

10   Death Signs

pp. 65–66   *Kate.* NEFA, (C): Mary Biscoe, Millinockett, Me., 1966.

pp. 66–67   *James Hardy.* Adapted from Creighton, *Magic*, pp. 6–7, Nova Scotia.

p. 67   *Second sight.* Creighton, *Ghosts*, pp. 69–70, Nova Scotia.

pp. 67–68   Rockport, Maine. NEFA, (C): Carol Goodrich, Rockport, Me., 1966.

pp. 68–69   *St. Mark's Eve.* Blakesborough, pp. 77–78; Henderson, pp. 51–52; Harland, p. 229, all England.

pp. 69–70   *Other death signs: Picture,* general; *clock,* FCB 5052, 5057, 5058, North Carolina; *bird,* FCB 8558; *beetle,* Opie, *Lore,* p. 213, England; *coffin,* Hyatt 15096, Illinois; *jump rope rhyme,* Botkin, *New England,* p. 596, New England.

11   Apollo and the Pythia

"Oracle," pp. 1015–18; Loewe, pp. 96–100.

12   A Crystal Ball

p. 74   *Jeane Dixon.* Ellis, pp. 77–78, quoting Glass.

p. 75   *Using a crystal.* Various sources.

pp. 75–77 *Mamie Fish.* Adapted from a 1905 American account in Lehr, pp. 233–35. A similar story without names or places is one of the better-known legends regarding soothsaying.

pp. 77–78 *A crystal and a scryer.* Kittredge, pp. 185–203; Aubrey, pp. 154–58; Thomas, *Religion*, pp. 215–17, 230, 242.

pp. 78–79 *Jonas Rushford.* Adapted from Wesley, p. 472.

p. 80 *Telling the future.* Ellis, pp. 78–85, 104–20, England.

13   Your Future in an Egg

Henderson, p. 105, England; Hand, *Compendium*, 6492, 25137, 25169–74, Ohio, FCB 13068, North Carolina.

14   Astrology

p. 83 *Six teenagers in ten.* Gallup Youth Survey, June 6, 1984.

pp. 84–89 *Astrological signs.* General.

pp. 90–92 *Astrology in sixteenth and seventeenth centuries.* Thomas, *Religion*, pp. 285–356, 632, 645; MacKay, pp. 282–90.

pp. 93–95 *Casting a horoscope.* General. Seligmann, p. 372; Ellis, pp. 132–34, England.

p. 95 *Current trends.* Horn, pp. 23–24, United States; Ellis, pp. 141–42, England.

Bibliography

Books

Books that may be of interest to young people are marked with an asterisk (*).

*Abrahams, Roger D., ed. *Jump-Rope Rhymes: A Dictionary.* Austin, Tex.: University of Texas Press, 1969.

Addy, Sidney O. *Household Tales.* London: David Nutt, 1895. Reprint edition, Wakefield, Yorkshire, England: E.P. Publishing, Ltd., 1973.

Aubrey, John. *Miscellanies Upon Various Subjects,* 4th ed. London: John Russell Smith, 1857.

*Aylesworth, Thomas G. *Astrology and Foretelling the Future.* New York: Franklin Watts, 1973.

Bei, Ama. *How to Read Tea Leaves.* Rhinebeck, N.Y.: V. Near Publishing Co., 1934.

Blakesborough, Richard. *Wit, Character, Folklore and Custom of the North Riding of Yorkshire.* Salisbury-by-the-Sea, England: W. Rapp & Sons, 1911.

Botkin, Benjamin, ed. *Folksay.* Norman, Okla.: University of Oklahoma Press, 1930.

———, ed. *A Treasury of New England Folklore:* rev. ed. New York: Crown Publishers, Inc., 1965.

Bowness, Charles. *Romany Magic.* Northamptonshire, England: The Aquarium Press, 1973.

*Branley, Franklyn M. *Age of Aquarius: You and Astrology.* New York: Thomas Y. Crowell, 1979.

The Frank C. Brown Collection of North Carolina Folklore, Vol. 5. Durham, N.C.: Duke University Press, 1952.

Coffin, Tristram P., and Hennig Cohen. *Folklore in America.* Garden City, N.Y.: Doubleday & Company, 1966.

*Cohen, Daniel. *The Magic Art of Foretelling the Future.* New York: Dodd, Mead & Company, 1973.

Creighton, Helen, ed. *Bluenose Ghosts.* Toronto: The Ryerson Press, 1957.

————. *Bluenose Magic.* Toronto: The Ryerson Press, 1968.

Ellis, Keith. *Prediction and Prophecy.* London: Wayland Publishers, 1973.

Encyclopedia of the Occult Sciences. New York: Robert M. McBride and Company, n.d. Reprint ed., Detroit: Gale Research Co., 1972.

Encyclopedia of Superstition, Folklore and the Occult Sciences. Milwaukee: J. H. Yewdale and Sons, 1903. Reprint ed., Detroit: Gale Research Co., 1971.

*Gallant, Roy A. *Astrology: Sense or Nonsense.* Garden City, N.Y.: Doubleday & Company, Inc., 1974.

Gardner, Emelyn E. *Folklore from the Schoharie Hills, New York.* Ann Arbor, Mich.: University of Michigan Press, 1937.

Gibson, Walter B., and Litzka R. Gibson. *The Complete Illustrated Book of Divination and Prophecy.* Garden City, N.Y.: Doubleday & Company, Inc., 1973.

Glass, Justine. *The Story of Fulfilled Prophecy.* London: Cassell, 1969.

119

*Gray, Eden. *The Tarot Revealed: A Modern Guide to Reading the Tarot Cards.* New York: Bell Publishing Company, 1960.

Hand, Wayland D., ed. "Popular Beliefs and Superstitions," *The Frank C. Brown Collection of North Carolina Folklore,* Vols. 6, 7. Durham, N.C.: Duke University Press, 1961.

Hand, Wayland D. et al., eds. *Popular Beliefs and Superstitions: A Compendium of American Folklore.* Vols. 1, 2. Boston: G. K. Hall and Company, 1981. 3 vols. Some 36,209 beliefs from the Ohio collections of the folklorist Newbell Niles Puckett.

Harland, John, and T. T. Wilkinson. *Lancashire Legends.* London: George Routledge and Sons, 1873.

Henderson, William. *Notes on the Folk Lore of the Northern Counties of England and the Borders.* London: Longmans, Green, and Co., 1866.

Hyatt, Harry M. *Folklore from Adams County, Ill.* 2nd and rev. ed. New York: Memoirs of the Alma Egan Hyatt Foundation, 1965.

*Jennings, Gary. *Black Magic, White Magic.* New York: The Dial Press, 1964.

*Johnson, Clifton. *What They Say in New England and Other American Folklore.* Boston: Lee and Shepherd, 1896. Reprint ed., Carl A. Withers, ed. New York: Columbia University Press, 1963.

Jones, William. *Credulities Past and Present.* London: Chatto and Windus, 1880.

*Kettelcamp, Larry. *Astrology: Wisdom of the Stars.* New York: William Morrow and Company, 1973.

*————. *Dreams*. New York: William Morrow and Company, 1968.

Kittredge, George. *Witchcraft in Old and New England.* Cambridge, Mass.: Harvard University Press, 1929. Reprint ed., New York: Atheneum Publishers, 1972.

Knapp, Mary, and Herbert Knapp. *One Potato, Two Potato . . . : The Secret Education of American Children.* New York: W.W. Norton & Company, Inc., 1976.

Lehr, Elizabeth Drexel. *"King Lehr" and the Gilded Age.* Philadelphia: J.B. Lippincott Co., 1935.

Loewe, Michael, and Carmen Blacker, eds. *Divination and Oracles.* London: George Allen & Unwin, 1981.

MacKay, Charles. *Memoirs of Extraordinary Popular Delusions and the Madness of Crowds.* London: Richard Bentley, 1841. Reprint ed., New York: Farrar, Straus and Giroux, 1932.

McNeill, F. Marion. *Hallowe'en: Its Origins and Ceremonies in the Scottish Tradition.* Edinburgh, Scotland: The Albyn Press, n.d.

Miall, Agnes M. *The Book of Fortune Telling.* London: Hamlyn Publishing Group, 1973.

*Milne, A.A. *When We Were Very Young.* New York: E.P. Dutton & Company, 1961.

Newell, William Wells. *Games and Songs of American Children.* New York: Harper & Brothers, 1883. Reprint ed., New York: Dover Publications, 1963.

Northcote, W. Thomas. *Crystal Gazing.* New York: Dodge Publishing Co., 1905.

Opie, Iona, and Peter Opie. *The Lore and Language of Schoolchildren.* London: Oxford University Press, 1959.

————, eds. *Oxford Dictionary of Nursery Rhymes*. Oxford, England: Oxford University Press, 1951.

Randolph, Vance. *Ozark Superstitions*. New York: Columbia University Press, 1947. Reprint ed., *Ozark Magic and Folklore*, New York: Dover Publications, Inc., 1964.

————, ed. *Who Blowed Up the Church House? And Other Ozark Folk Tales*. New York: Columbia University Press, 1952.

Sackett, S.J., and William E. Koch. *Kansas Folklore*. Lincoln, Nebr.: University of Nebraska Press, 1961.

Saxon, Lyle et al. of the Louisiana Writers' Project. *Gumbo Ya-Ya*. Boston: Houghton Mifflin Company, 1945.

*Schwartz, Alvin. *Cross Your Fingers, Spit in Your Hat: Superstitions and Other Beliefs*. New York: J.B. Lippincott Co., 1974.

*————. *Scary Stories to Tell in the Dark*. New York: J.B. Lippincott Co., 1981.

Seligmann, Kurt. *The History of Magic*. New York: Pantheon Books, 1948. Reprint ed., *Magic, Supernaturalism and Religion*. New York: Pantheon Books, 1976.

Thomas, Daniel L., and Lucy B. Thomas. *Kentucky Superstitions*. Princeton, N.J.: Princeton University Press, 1920.

Thomas, Keith. *Religion and the Decline of Magic*. New York: Macmillan Publishing Co., 1971.

*Thomson, Peggy. *On Reading Palms*. Englewood Cliffs, N.J.: Prentice-Hall, Inc., 1974.

Waite, Arthur Edward. *The Occult Sciences*. London: K. Paul, Trench, Trubner & Co., 1923. Reprint of an 1891 work.

122

Wesley, The Rev. John. *The Journal of the Rev. John Wesley, A.M.* Standard edition, Vol. 4. London: The Epworth Press, 1938.

Whitney, Annie W., and Caroline C. Bullock. *Folklore from Maryland.* MAFS, Vol. 18. New York: American Folklore Society, 1925.

Articles

Bancroft, Carol. "Folklore of the Central City District." *CFQ* 4 (1945):315–42.

Brandt, Anthony. "Looking for an Answer." *Esquire* 101 (January 1984):18.

Chou, Hung-hsiang. "Chinese Oracle Bones." *Scientific American* 240 (April 1979):135–42.

"Dandelion Seed Prognostication." *WF* 12 (1953):52.

DeCrow, Gertrude. "Folklore from Maine." *JAF* 5 (1892):318.

"Dreams." *International Encyclopedia of the Social Sciences.* New York: Crowell-Collier and Macmillan, Inc., 1968.

Hand, Wayland D. "The Folklore, Customs, and Traditions of the Butte Miner." *CFQ* 5 (1946):1–25.

Horn, Patricia. "Scientists Look to the Stars and Find Them False." *Psychology Today* 9 (February 1976):23–24.

Kell, Katharine T. "The Folklore of the Daisy," Part 3. *JAF* 69 (1956):369–76.

Lewis, Linda. "Did You Ever Swing on a Star?" *Atlantic* 238 (July 1976):76–81.

Moore, Omar K. "Divination—a New Perspective." *AA* 59 (1957):69–74.

"Oracle." *Encyclopedia Britannica*, 1972, Vol. 16:1015–18.

Prose, Francine. "Telling Fortunes." *New York Times*, April 11, 1985, p. C2.

Roberts, Hilda. "Louisiana Superstitions." *JAF* 40 (1927):144–208.

Smiley, Portia. "Folklore from the South." *JAF* 32 (1919):357–83.

Weiss, Harvey B. "Oneirocritica Americana." *New York Public Library Bulletin* 48 (June 1944):519–41, 642–53.

Index

aces (cards), 41–43
ancestors, answers from, 54
animals, 10, 11, 12, 61–64
Apollo, 71–73, 106–7
apple, 14; seeds of, 16–17, 21
Aquarius, 88
Arab priests, divination, 104
Aries, 85
Artemidorus Daldianus, 60
ascendant, in horoscope, 94
astrology, 83–95; teenagers and, 108
augurs, Roman, 102

baby, dream of, 61
Babylonia, 83, 89–91
baldness, dream of, 61
basement, dream of, 62
basket, dream of, 62
bat, dream of, 62
bed, omen, 10
birds, death signs, 69
birthdate, astrological sign, 84–89

birthdays, omens, 10, 101
books of dreams, 60
bridge, dream of, 62
bubbles, on top of tea, 32

Cancer, 86
Capricorn, 88
cards, reading of, 38–45
casting lots, 24–25, 104–5
cat, 10; dream of, 62
cauliflower, dream of, 62
cemetery, dream of, 62
children, number of, 21
China, oracle bones, 54–55, 105
clock, death sign, 69
cloud, dream of, 62
clubs (cards), 42
coffin, dream of, 58–59, 62
comb, count of teeth, 25
cootie catcher, 33–37
Crowther, Jonathan, 78–79
crystal balls, 74–80, 107
cures, by dreams, 105

daisy: petals, 15, 16–17; seeds, 21

dandelion, 62; seeds, 20

death signs, 65–70; dream, 62

Delphi, oracle of, 71, 106

destiny line, in hand, 52–53

diamonds (cards), 42, 43

dice, predictions from, 26

dirt, 11, 101

ditches, 11, 101

divination, 8

Dixon, Jeane, 74, 107

doctors, astrologers as, 91

Dodona, temple of Zeus at, 106–7

dog, omen, 11

drawing lots, 24–27, 104–5

dream books, 60

Dreams (Kettelcamp), 59

dream signs, 57–64, 105–6

dumb supper, 18–19

ear, omen, 11

eating, dream of, 62

eggs: dream of, 62; future told by, 81–82

ephemeris, 94

ESP (extrasensory perception), 107; teenagers and, 108

falling, dream of, 63

fate line, in hand, 52–53

fingers, marriage prospect, 19

fire, dream of, 63

fish, dream of, 63

Fish, Mamie, 75–77

flooded mine, dream of, 58

flowers, 11; dreams, 63, 64

footsteps, death sign, 66–67

friend, dream of, 63

funeral, 11; dream of, 63

future, prediction of, 7–8, 80

Gemini, 85–86

gods, 9; Babylonian, 89–92; Greek, 71–73, 106–7

gold, dream of, 63

Gray, Eden, The Tarot Revealed, 45

Greece, ancient, 104; dream cures, 105–6; gods, 106–7; oracles, 71–73

Hades, 106

hair, 11, 15–16, dream of, 63

Halloween: love magic, 18; mashed potatoes, 27

hand: marriage prospects, 19; omen, 11; reading of, 46–53

head line, in hand, 51–52

heart line, in hand, 51

hearts (cards), 41

Hera, 106

hills, dream of, 62

Hippocrates, 106

Hitler, Adolf, 84

holes, 11, 101

horoscopes, 83, 91–95

horse, 11; dream of, 63

house, dream of, 59; in horoscope, 93–94

hunters, oracle bones, 55–56

imitative magic, 108

initial of true love, 14–15

ink, crystal gazing, 77

insect: death sign, 69; dream
  of, 61; omens, 10, 12
interpretation of dream, 61–64

Japan, dream cure, 105
journey, dream of, 63
jump rope rhymes, 15, 70

Kettelcamp, Larry, *Dreams*, 59,
  60
keys, dream of, 63
king, dream of, 63
kisses, dream of, 63
knives, omen, 12
knocking sounds, 65–66

Labrador, oracle bones, 55–56
ladder, omen, 12
Leo, 86
letter, dream of, 63
Libra, 87
life line, in palm of hand, 50
life-style, 22–23
Lincoln, Abraham, 57–58, 60
lines, in palm of hand, 49–53
lion, dream of, 63
lots, casting, 24–27, 104–5
love magic, 14–23, 102–4

M, in palm of hand, 50
magic, 97, 108
Major Arcana (tarot), 44–45
maps, from oracle bones, 55
marriage prediction, 15–23, 39
Mars, Plain of, in hand, 53
MASH, 103–4
mashed potatoes, 27
matching names, 17–18, 23

meanings of dreams, 61–64
medicine, by astrologers, 91
Milne, A. A., "Lines and
  Squares," 101
mine flooding, dream of, 58
missing persons, crystal ball to
  find, 78
money, dream of, 64
moon, new, 12; love magic, 18
mounts, in palm of hand, 48–
  49
mud, dream of, 64
music, dream of, 64

nails, 11, 101
names, matching of, 17–18, 23
Naskapi Indians, 55–56
New Year's Eve, 69
nine cards, 40–43
nose, 12

Old Testament divination, 104
Olympian gods, 106–7
omens, 9–11, 101–2
oracle bones, 54–56, 105
oracles, 71–73, 106–7

page in book, 25
palm reading, 46–53
parapsychology, 107
pebble, ripples from, 25
personal problems, astrological
  advice, 91
picture, falling from wall, 69
pig, omen, 12
Pisces, 89
PK (psychokinesis), 107
Plain of Mars, in hand, 53

planets, positions of, 94–95
Poseidon, 106
precognition, 107
premonitions, 69
priest, divination by, 104
priestess, oracle of Delphi, 72–73
psychokinesis (PK), 107
Pythia, 73, 106

queen, dream of, 64
queens (cards), 41–43

rhymes: death prediction, 70; love magic, 15, 16–17, 103; omens, 10, 11
ring, marriage prediction, 15–16
river, dream of, 64
Roman augurs, 102
Rushford, Jonas, 78–79

Sagittarius, 87–88
Saint Agnes' Eve, 18
Saint Mark's Eve, 68–69
Scorpio, 87
scryers, 78
second sight, 67–68
shoelace, knotted, 13
sky charts, 90–92
snake, dream of, 64
sneeze, 13
socks, omen, 13
spades, (cards), 43
spiders, 13

stars, positions of, 94–95
stone, skipping of, 21
success of marriage, 23
surface for crystal gazing, 77

tarot cards, 44–45
Tarot Revealed, The (Gray), 45
Taurus, 85
tea leaves, reading of, 28–32
teenagers and fortune telling, 107–8
teeth, dream of, 64
telling of dreams, 61
tens (cards), 41–43
thief: dream of, 64; to find, 78
thumb, marriage outlook, 19
time, and vision of future, 80
toes, string tied to, 20
trump cards (tarot), 44–45
tunnel, dream of, 64

vegetables, dream of, 64
Virgo, 86–87

Walsh, Vincent, 75–77
water, dream of, 64
word, letter count, 25
words in crowd, 25, 104
World War II, astrologers, 84
wrinkles, number of children predicted by, 21
wrists, 13; lines on, 50

yes/no, 24–27, 38–39, 104–5

Zeus, 106–7